All About Strange Beasts
of the Present

All About
Strange Beasts
of the Present

By **Robert S. Lemmon**

Illustrated by **Rudolf Freund**

RANDOM HOUSE
NEW YORK

Contents

The face of the earth . . . .

1

Our
Amazing World

It is hard to believe that at this very minute a lizard with changeable colors is catching insects with the end of a tongue as long as its body. Close to the bottom of a river, too, a fish is defending itself by jolting its enemies with built-in electric shocks. In the tropics an almost brainless mammal is spending a large part of its life upside down. And in another part of the earth a queer, furry, leathery-beaked animal with poisonous spurs on its hind legs is laying eggs!

These are only a few of the strange beasts which you can see in the world today. All of them are very much alive although they may appear too astonishing to be real. But a great many years from now a lot of them will have vanished forever. Those kinds which remain will probably be so changed that you would hardly recognize them. We know that this will happen because dozens of scientists have proved that nearly every living thing is always turning into something a little different or disappearing entirely. The earth itself is constantly changing too.

Dinosaurs roamed the earth 100 million years ago.

Of course, these changes take place very, very slowly. Hundreds, thousands, perhaps a million years may pass before we can be sure about them. But they keep going on just the same.

For example, millions of years ago, in the days of dinosaurs and other strange beasts of the past, the earth was not at all like the earth today. In certain regions there were oceans instead of the great deserts which we have now. Some of our highest mountains had not even appeared above the surface of enormous flat, marshy plains. Others, which now are no bigger than ordinary hills, were as tall as the famous Alps of Switzerland. There were whole continents where now there are only deep-water islands.

The changes of climate have been tremendous, too. At one time the northern United States and northern Europe were as warm as the tropics. Later, these regions were covered four different times with vast sheets of ice called glaciers. These came down from the Far North and lasted for a long, long time. They made the whole country bitterly cold. There was no summer weather at all.

Those terrible "deep freezes" occurred during the Pleistocene Period, which began about a hundred million years ago. Each visit of the glaciers lasted for many thousands of years. In between them there were even longer stretches of fairly warm weather. But the glaciers were so huge and bitterly cold that we call this part of the earth's history the Ice Age.

On many hilltops as far south as New York City, you can still see grooves and scratches made by glaciers on the surface of large, exposed masses of rock. They were cut by hard stones frozen tight in the bottom of the ice sheets. As the mighty glaciers crept down from the polar regions, their weight forced these stones to grind into everything they came to. Some of the largest grooves are eight inches deep and fifteen inches wide. Many of the glacial scars which you see today run from north to south. Others extend from east to west. Each of them shows the direction in which a particular glacier was moving.

Such important changes in land, water and climate were dangerous to all living things. Plants and animals cannot live unless they are able to get along well in their particular surroundings, or *environment*. So, when an environment changes, they simply must do something about it. Otherwise they are likely to die out forever.

One way to escape such a fate, at least for a while, is to move to some other part of the earth where conditions are more like those which used to exist in the old homes. Some authorities believe that many of our birds met the hardships of the Ice Age by flying southward to warmer lands.

Other creatures, and various kinds of plants, were saved by changing themselves gradually so as to keep in step with the differences which came in the climate. Some grew larger, others smaller. We ourselves are much taller, slimmer and straighter than our early ancestors who lived in the Ice Age. Certain kinds of plants as well as animals developed special formations which made it possible for them to survive in the new, dry deserts, for example. A few stayed pretty much as they were and managed to get along all right. These were the really tough ones. They could adapt themselves to changing conditions more easily than most of their neighbors.

The earth and its inhabitants never stood perfectly still in those bygone ages. They are not standing still today. But I think there will always be living beasts of different kinds as fantastic as the wildest dream.

2

In the United States and Canada

On Land

The northwest part of our continent is full of surprises. There are hundreds of lakes and a network of big and little rivers on both sides of the Canadian border and on through Alaska. Dense evergreen forests cover thousands of square miles. Several of the countless mountains tower more than three miles above the level of the sea. These and many other peaks are snow-capped even in summer. In winter the temperature drops far below zero and stays there for weeks. The snow continues to fall until even the windows of the lonely trappers' cabins are completely buried. Altogether, it is a part of the world in which you would expect almost anything exciting to happen.

The vast forested stretches of this natural wonderland are the home of the wolverine, a strange beast if ever there was one. It is not related to wolves, in spite of its name. Instead it is a cousin of the minks, weasels and other members of the Mustellidae family. But it is much, much smarter, meaner and tougher than they are. The Indians and other fur trappers fear and hate it because it makes their lives very miserable indeed.

In some ways, wolverines make you think of small bears. They seldom weigh more than thirty pounds or so, but their thick, glossy, dark brown fur makes them look bigger than that. Their feet are bearlike and armed with long, curved, wicked-looking claws. Some people call them skunk-bears. This is because they often hoist their bushy tails straight up in the air like a skunk.

A wolverine's jaws and teeth are remarkably powerful. So are his short thick legs. His beady black eyes look hard and cruel. Other much larger animals are afraid of him. A wolverine has been known to kill and eat even full-grown deer and moose that were stuck in

The wolverine is the big boss of the north woods.

deep snow. He is truly the big boss of the big woods.

Wolverines eat almost anything they can find, especially if it smells like meat. They are so very wary that men seldom see them. In winter they will follow a woodsman's trap line for miles, stealing every bait without getting caught themselves. They often break into his cabin, too, while he is away. Once inside, they rip open and ruin everything they can find. Blankets are shredded, bacon eaten, flour bags spilled and scattered in all directions. The whole place looks as if a cyclone had struck it. Outside, even supplies that have been carefully packed and stored on tall poles or high in the trees are pulled apart and destroyed.

Why are wolverines so destructive? The only answer seems to be that they have the world's meanest and ugliest dispositions. For their size they are probably the toughest fighters among all our North American wild animals. And they act as if they know it!

Besides their home in the forested regions of the Northwest, these astonishing beasts are occasionally found all the way across upper Canada to the Atlantic side. They used to range farther down into the United States too. This explains why the name "Wolverine State" was given to Michigan. But as the forests gave way to more and more farms and towns, the environment changed. The wolverines could not stand this, so they retreated farther and farther northward. They are rough, tough fellows. And they get along best in rough, tough, lonesome places.

The lynx trails its prey craftily and without making a sound.

Through much of the forested wolverine country, and farther south in the Rocky Mountains, you may also find the Canada lynx. Its habits and appearance are entirely different from those of the skunk-bear. That beast depends on his strength, suspicion and bad temper.

But a lynx is a true cat and behaves like one. It hunts mostly at night, trailing its prey craftily and without making a sound. Finally there is a swift rush, a pounce, and often that spells the end for a snowshoe hare, grouse or perhaps a baby fawn.

Unlike most of the cat tribe, a lynx has only a stump of a tail. He makes up for this though by wearing a long fringe of hair on both cheeks and across his throat. He looks as though he has bushy but well-brushed side whiskers and beard. On the tip of each ear there is a long, slim tuft of black hair which makes you think of an artist's pencil paintbrush. From this fuzzy frame his big yellow eyes stare at you steadily. In sunlight their pupils are only black slits, like those of tame cats. But as dusk comes, they grow bigger and rounder in order to let in more light. By the time it is fully dark, they seem to take up most of the eye space. No wonder a cat can see so well at night!

Because lynxes are North-country beasts, they are well equipped to stand the cold. Their pale, brownish-gray fur is more than an inch thick in winter. Even their long legs are covered with this perfect blanket. And all around their surprisingly large feet the hair is so dense that it provides its wearer with four first-class snowshoes.

All About Strange Beasts of the Present

A fully grown male lynx is far bigger than any domestic cat. He may be more than three feet long from nose tip to tail tip, and two feet from the ground to the top of his shoulders. When well fed he sometimes weighs almost forty pounds, and he can squall as loud as ten ordinary tomcats put together. Yet, while still very young, he is as cute and playful as any tame kitten.

These Canada lynxes are excellent climbers and spend much of their time in trees. Most of their hunting, though, is done on the ground. Often the old ones stalk their prey alone. But the youngsters stay with their mother for months, and during this stage the family goes hunting together. They have a clever method of moving through the woods in a sort of skirmish line. This gives them a much better chance of finding and catching a meal than if they traveled singly. You would be right if you called this habit a perfect example of good teamwork.

Heavily wooded mountain country is the favorite

The tracks of the Canada lynx spell danger for other animals.

territory of these big, handsome wild cats. In winter, however—especially if the supply of snowshoe hares gets low in the forests—they will range northward onto the open tundra where there are no real trees at all. When the temperature drops to fifty below zero, a fellow just has to find food—or else. And nobody knows this better than a Canada lynx.

Many parts of the Rocky Mountains are so high that all the trees are very small. Wolverines and lynxes seldom go there. One reason for this is that their special kinds of food are scarce in such places. Every wild creature stays in the environment where it can live best and most safely.

Yet these harsh, rugged peaks are far from deserted. Numerous mice and other small rodents hide among the boulders and come out to feed on the low-growing plants near by. There are a few kinds of really large mammals, too, such as the bighorn sheep. These relatives of our domestic sheep are so big that if you have good eyes you can see them at a long distance. They will see you too! If you should try to get much closer, they will escape in a manner that leaves you gasping with astonishment. They can do it only because of the special way they are built.

An old bighorn ram may be three and one-half feet

Hoofs of the bighorn sheep give them a grip on any rock surface.

high at the shoulder and weigh 250 pounds or more. The ewes, or females, are a little smaller. All of them—rams, ewes and young lambs—have marvelous rock-climbing hoofs and know exactly how to use them.

The bottom of each of these two-toed hoofs looks like a pair of oblong, tough, black rubber cups. Each cup has a sharp, much harder rim. This non-skid sole can get a firm grip on practically any rock surface. The sheep's stocky, strong-boned ankles and legs are extremely nimble and powerful too. This combination of feet and muscles makes it possible for the bighorn to leap from boulder to boulder with breath-taking speed. Also, it can easily go up or down a precipice steeper than the steepest house roof. And it calmly walks along lofty ledges almost too narrow for you to see.

Bighorns eat the grass and other vegetation in the high mountain basins and valleys. Usually these places lie between the snow line and a point a little below timber line. This is also the region where the old rams fight their thunderous battles for leadership of the flocks during the mating season.

In preparation for these encounters, they choose a piece of level ground where they can face each other at a distance of ten or fifteen feet. Suddenly and at the same instant both of them charge forward with lowered heads. Their huge curved horns meet with a crash that can be heard far away. Often the force of the collision throws both battlers back on their hind legs. But they keep on charging and crashing until one or the other decides that he has been beaten.

Perhaps you wonder why neither ram breaks his neck or his horns in these wild battles. As for the neck, it is protected by a special, extremely strong rubber-like reinforcement at the danger spot where it joins the skull. The horns are safe because the blow is always struck with their thickest central part. Their thinner, curving points are entirely outside the danger zone.

There are several somewhat different forms of these American mountain sheep. One, with all-white hair, lives in Alaska. In the same region there are gray as well as blackish fellows with light-colored rumps. Farther south, in our American Rockies, there is the regular brown, white-rumped bighorn with blackish lower legs.

Some authorities believe that the ancient ancestors of these splendidly rugged beasts lived among the Altai Mountains of western Mongolia. Some of the strongest ones probably reached America by crossing the land bridge which once connected the continent of Asia with

Every wild creature is afraid to tackle the porcupine.

Alaska. Others are believed to have spread southward from Mongolia to India and northern Africa. Whether or not all this actually happened, it is certainly true that mountain sheep of this general type now have a range which reaches nearly halfway around the globe.

Below timber line in the Rockies there is an odd, very different mammal, the porcupine. He and his relatives also have a tremendous range in the Old World as well as the New. Our American species is at home in most of the forested areas of the United States, Alaska and Canada. About the only regions without him are the open plains of the West, the Midwest, and the whole section south of New York City.

Back-country people often call the porcupine a quill-pig. He certainly is covered with slender quills. Also, he is as stupid, clumsy and generally slow-moving as any pig. But actually he is a rodent, with gnawing teeth somewhat like a rabbit's or squirrel's. Yet nearly every other wild creature in the woods is afraid to attack him.

The reason for this fear is easy to understand. From nose to tail tip, a distance of thirty inches or so, the blackish hair on his sides and upper parts is thickly sprinkled with stiff, needlesharp spines from half an inch to four inches long. There may be as many as 20,-000 or 25,000 of these peculiar weapons. As soon as any of them are lost, new ones grow quickly to replace them.

Many people believe that a porcupine can shoot his spines or quills whenever he wants to. This is not true. The real facts of the case are still more strange.

An undisturbed porcupine usually goes his clumsy way with his spines lowered and partly hidden by the hair. Each one is loosely anchored in special muscles just under the skin. At the first sign of danger these muscles snap all the quills into an erect position and hold them there.

Most of a porcupine's natural enemies attack with their mouths. So, if "porky" thinks that a wolf or fox is about to make a dive for him, he does a very smart thing. At the last moment he whirls around so that his back is toward his foe. This brings the longest quills into the ready position. Only a foolish or very hungry animal will push his face into a spiny barricade like that. If he does, his head, muzzle and the inside of his open mouth will be stuck full of vicious little spears. Every one of them lets go of the porcupine and goes into the attacker. Even his throat will get a dose of them, for porcupines have a neat trick of slapping their tails upward and hitting this important unprotected spot.

Once a quill gets its point through an enemy's skin, it stays there. The harder the victim tries to shake or

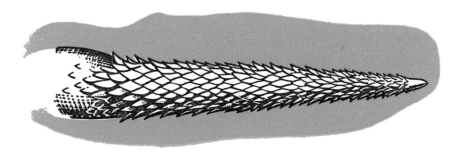

The porcupine's quill has many backward-pointing barbs.

scratch it out, the deeper it goes. This is because each quill tip has several dozen tiny, overlapping, backward-pointing barbs. These little hooks pull the quill farther into the sufferer every time he moves. Some of the quills may finally puncture important arteries and even the heart itself. A strong human pull with a pair of pliers, soon after the fight, is about the only way to get them out.

Surprisingly enough, quill-pigs are first-rate swimmers. They steam along quite high in the water too. This is because all their thousands of yellowish, black-tipped quills are hollow and full of air which helps keep their owners afloat.

The porcupine does most of his feeding high up in trees, especially hemlocks. There he gnaws away steadily on the tender bark and young shoots. He is crazy about salt too. Often he will chew an empty pork barrel, just to get the salt which has soaked into it. He will even gnaw a shovel or hoe handle which has absorbed salty perspiration from a farmer's hands on a hot summer day. But whatever happens, about the only word he ever utters is a grunt or a mutter.

Few mammals, except occasionally the porcupine, ever go near a village. There is another much smaller beast,

With legs spread, the flying squirrel can glide through the air.

however, which does not mind people and houses. This is the unbelievable flying squirrel. The northern species lives in Canada and the upper parts of the United States. He has an almost identical cousin who usually replaces him from the Great Lakes to the Gulf of Mexico. Both of them are quite common in some town parks as well as the suburban and country woods.

Flying squirrels have no wings to flap so they cannot fly as birds do. But they can glide slantingly downward through the air for a hundred feet or more. They do this by means of a curious strip of loose skin which connects their front and hind feet on both sides. While the squirrel is climbing and jumping about among the branches of a tree, these twin flaps are just wrinkles along the sides of his body. But when he wants to take off for another tree, he simply leaps into the air, spreads his four legs wide to expand the flaps, and away he goes.

Flying squirrels are active only at night. During the day they sleep in tree holes or perhaps the abandoned leaf nests of larger squirrels. At dusk they come out, their big, night-seeing eyes all ready for action. They delight in dashing around in the treetops and coasting downward on their marvelous "wings." Frequently on pleasant summer nights a crowd of them will gather and put on a sort of jumping and sailing carnival, apparently just for fun.

One of these beautiful little brown-and-white fellows weighs only about five ounces. Its soft, plumy tail is quite flat and nearly as long as the body and head together. When used as a rudder and stabilizer, it helps the squirrel to make sudden sharp turns in mid-air. It also is a first-class muffler for cold paws in winter. And many a flying squirrel has the habit of sleeping with his tail laid across his eyes as if to shut out the light.

Flying squirrels make jolly pets, especially the young ones. They quickly learn their way around the house and become perfectly tame in a few days. Every room, closet and clothes pocket is daintily explored, for they have endless curiosity about new places. Yet this does not prevent their taking plenty of time to keep their fluffy fur perfectly clean and combed with their tiny claws.

Few people ever see flying squirrels, even though they may be common in the neighborhood. The reason is that they move around only after dark and are very quiet. Sometimes, though, you can catch a glimpse of one in broad daylight. The way to do this is to rap sharply on the trunk of some old tree in which there is a hole, perhaps made by a woodpecker. One or more flying squirrels may be sleeping in that dark retreat. If so, the rapping will generally make them stick their heads out of the opening to see what's going on.

At Home in the Water

An entirely different mammal, the river otter, can be found in an area almost as large as the flying squirrel's. You may see one in unsettled regions almost anywhere in Canada from Labrador to the tip of Alaska. On our side of the border, these otters range practically all over the United States except parts of the far South-west. Wherever they go, they seem to get more fun out of life than any other wild animal I know.

River otters are as much at home in the water as on land. An especially large one is close to four feet long. About one-third of this length is a tapered tail with a thick base. This serves as a perfect rudder for fast swimming turns. The entire animal is covered by thick, glossy fur that is just about waterproof. Its color is rich brown, a little paler on the cheeks and throat.

Otters are born with a great love of play. Young as well as old ones join in long games of follow-the-leader and hide-and-seek. These chases may take them into the water, among trees and bushes on shore, or both. Another popular sport is sliding downhill on their stomachs. This tobogganing works equally well in snow and slippery mud. The faster the slide, the better the coasters like it. It is great sport, too, to throw good-sized pebbles into deep water and try to catch them before they touch bottom.

A river otter eats many kinds of small creatures. Some of his favorites are fish, fresh-water clams, snails, crawfish, big insects, lizards and snakes. He can swim under water for a quarter of a mile without coming up for air. His webbed feet and tail rudder give him such speed and control that sometimes he can outswim even a trout. Most of the fish, though, are caught under rocks where they have taken refuge.

Extremely cold winters may make serious trouble for otters by completely freezing the surface of streams and lakes. Unless they can find holes in the ice, they can neither get into the water to catch fish nor come up for the occasional fresh air which they need. About the only thing they can do about it is to hunt for some place where there is a bit of open water. This may mean a long journey. I once tracked an otter for nearly three miles through snow eight inches deep. His favorite small river was completely icebound. So, as his trail showed, he had left it and headed across country over a high ridge to another larger and swifter stream. There he found a few open holes through which he could go fishing. I'm sure he caught plenty to eat, because that is a stream where I have had good fishing luck during the summer.

These river otters have larger, much fatter cousins called sea otters. They live in salt water along the California coast. Much of the time they loaf lazily on their backs in beds of floating kelp, which is a kind of coarse

The sea otter cracks clams against rocks placed on his chest.

seaweed. Their principal food is clams and other shell-fish. They catch these on the sandy bottom below the kelp. In order to break the hardest shells of their meals they also bring up fair-sized pieces of rock which they place on their chests as they float face up. Then, gripping the stubborn clam with their front paws, they bang it down on the stone until the shell breaks and they can get at the soft meat inside. One authority who has made a close study of sea otters has watched this astonishing procedure many times. She has photographed it too. So we know just how it is done.

These cheerful, easy-going beasts eat three regular meals a day—in the morning, about noon and toward evening. In between they seldom take a single bite.

The snapping turtle is certainly one of the ugliest of the fresh-water dwellers. You may find one in almost any sluggish stream, pond or lake in southeast Canada and all over the United States as far west as the Rockies.

Snappers look as if they had just crawled out of a nightmare. Their horny upper shells or *carapaces* are nearly black and sometimes spotted with growing moss. When they lumber along on land, their thick, leathery

A big snapping turtle may reach a weight of sixty pounds.

legs hold the lower shell or *plastron* well above the ground. A row of sawtooth points runs along the top of the long tail. Up front there is a strong, collapsible neck that carries a vicious-looking head and bony, hooked snout. A big snapping turtle may live for more than a century and reach a weight of over sixty pounds.

Snappers look slow and awkward. But actually they can move with deadly speed. When looking for food near the bottom of a pond, they can leap forward like lightning to catch a fish or frog. Also, the long neck and wicked head can dart out and grab a victim faster than your eyes can follow them. A thirty-pounder can cut through a broom handle with a single snap of his sharp-edged jaws. He could do the same thing to a careless human finger or maybe a wrist!

This fabulous beast will eat practically any kind of flesh it can get. One favorite food is a young duck. The snapper simply rises slowly through the water below the unsuspecting bird, grabs it by a leg, and takes it to the bottom to be torn apart and swallowed in chunks. Even fully grown ducks occasionally suffer the same fate.

You really have to see a live snapping turtle to realize how repulsive it is. I had such an opportunity one spring

day while fishing a swampy creek. As I stood on the
bank, a whopping old snapper came floating down-
stream toward me. He was so near the surface that his
back and head were out of water. Now and then he
took a slow steering stroke with one leg. As he drifted
past, only a couple of yards away, he turned his head
and gave me the coldest, most cruel glare I have ever

A hungry skunk will dig out the eggs of a snapping turtle.

received. Probably he decided that I was only a motionless old stump, because he continued quietly on his way. But he certainly wasn't taking any chances—or missing any.

In May or June the female snapping turtles leave their watery homes to lay eggs in well-drained, often sunny spots on shore. You sometimes see one crawling across a country road on this important journey. When she finds a suitable place, she scrapes out a big hole with her hind legs and lays a couple of dozen round, white eggs in it. Then she covers them with loose soil, drags her plastron over this to make it firm and smooth, goes back to the pond, and never returns to see how the nest is getting along. Unless a hungry skunk digs up the eggs and eats them, they will hatch in about three months. As soon as the infant turtles can dig their way to the surface, they will instinctively head for the water to start living their own independent lives.

Fossil discoveries show that the turtle tribe was in existence 200,000,000 years ago. That was before the first dinosaurs appeared. Its members have changed somewhat since then of course. But their armored type of structure still remains in nearly every case. And they are probably as plentiful today as they ever were.

In the United States and Canada

In the Mississippi River region where snapping turtles are found, there is another beast that is hard to believe. This is the sprawling, hideous hellbender. It belongs to the reptile group, as does the snapper. But hellbenders are salamanders, not turtles. They are built a good deal like lizards.

A full-grown hellbender may measure two feet from the front of its broad flat head to the end of its slimy tail. Four stubby, crooked legs and big feet drag the creature along the bottoms of muddy streams on its hunt for worms, crawfish, water insects and other well-liked foods. It never comes out on dry land. Every inch of its loose, yellowish-brown to nearly black figure is completely homely. Its second name of mud puppy fits its shape very well indeed.

Few people except fishermen ever see hellbenders. This is because these beasts stick closely to the bottom, often hiding under rocks. Sometimes, however, they grab a hook baited for fish and are hauled to the surface. When this happens, the fisherman has a real job killing them, for they are as tough as they are horrid.

This peculiar salamander is perfectly adapted to the kind of life it leads. Probably it has few natural enemies. Also, a good-sized female lays as many as 450 eggs

A full-grown hellbender salamander may be two feet long.

every year so there are plenty of young hellbenders to
keep the population going. All salamanders lay eggs
from which *larvae* emerge. These underdeveloped
youngsters are called *newts*. A newt is what you might
call an imperfect stage. It must change considerably before it becomes just like its parents. Until this happens it
cannot lay eggs of its own.

But here is a remarkable fact about hellbender newts.

They never make this final change into different looking creatures, as all other salamander newts do. Instead, they remain "imperfect" all their lives. In spite of this, they are able to lay eggs when they get older.

The hellbender is the largest of the many kinds of salamanders in our northeastern states. But it is only a peewee compared with its five-foot Japanese cousin. A peculiar thing about this huge oriental relative is that it is found only in swift mountain streams some of which are so small that there is hardly enough water to cover it.

The story of these and other salamanders probably began 300,000,000 years ago. The chances are that their forebears were the first *vertebrate*, or backboned, animals to crawl ashore from the mighty seas of those prehistoric times. Some scientists believe that salamanders are closely related to the ancestral beasts from which, at a later date, the reptiles, birds and mammals developed.

One of the interesting things about the creatures of today is the enormous differences between many of them. And certainly no two are more startlingly different than the hellbender and the manatee or sea-cow. Both of them live in the water, but there the resemblance ends.

Manatees are grotesque, dark grayish beasts sometimes twelve or thirteen feet long and weighing almost a ton. Their shape reminds you a little of whales, but they are not related to those huge aquatic mammals. Their tails are like broad, rounded shovels. The head and body are joined by a short thick neck. The whole skin is covered with fine wrinkles and sprinkled with thin hairs.

A manatee's two front legs, or flippers, are paddle-like and grow quite low on its body. These flippers have shoulder, elbow and wrist joints and can move in all directions. Their ends, or hands, are used to push food toward the mouth. The head, especially when seen from the front, looks unbelievably strange. Its round, sad little eyes are set in heavy wrinkles. Below them is a tremendous, flat, bristly upper lip divided into two sections. These sections can move toward or away from each other as if they were a pair of jaws. This is a big help in placing food within reach of the actual mouth. Their owner hardly needs to use his lower lip at all.

These big, slow and completely harmless beasts feed on various kinds of water plants, often quite near

The manatee or sea-cow, a grotesque beast, weighs almost a ton.

the surface. Their front flippers reach out and gather bunches of the plants. Then, with the help of the hands and divided upper lip, the vegetable dinner is stuffed into the mouth. At mealtime the manatee's body floats quite upright in the water. The creature looks as though it is sitting at an invisible table.

Manatees prefer shallow water quite close to shore. Sometimes, however, they go out where it is much deeper. There they often arch their backbones, let their legs and tail ends hang down, and just take things easy. You have no idea how silly they look at such times. Once in a while they come up for air, then sink back again out of sight.

The best places to look for these curious sea-cows are the rivers of Florida, the West Indies, Mexico, Central America and northern South America. East of the Andes Mountains there is another, somewhat smaller species. And there is a third kind in West Africa. Scientists believe that all three were land mammals long, long ago. No one knows when or why they decided to take to the water and stay there.

In the broad ocean currents of the North American coast, the conditions are entirely different from those in the quiet home of the manatees. The water is so salty that most fresh-water animals cannot live in it. Storms sometimes whip up such mighty waves that their sides are like long, sloping hills.

Far below the surface there is almost full darkness. That is where great sperm whales sometimes have desperate battles with giant squids. Nowhere else in the

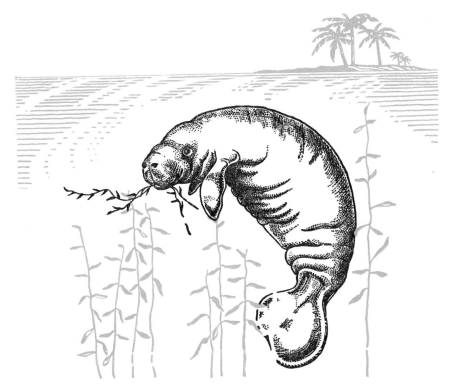

The flippers of the manatee help push food into its mouth.

world, I suppose, are such furious struggles fought by such enormous, fantastic beasts.

The square-headed sperm whale may be more than sixty feet long. His tremendous lower jaw is thickly set with teeth. He enjoys squid meat, and his throat is big enough to swallow a man whole. The whale is a vertebrate of course. But his giant squid opponent has no backbone and therefore is an *invertebrate*. This monstrous beast is also the largest known invertebrate in the world. When the fight is over, the skin around the whale's head will be severely spotted with raw wounds made by the suction discs on the squid's ten arms or *tentacles*. And probably several of the squid's arms will have been chopped off by the whale's powerful jaw.

A giant squid's body can be as long as eight feet. He usually moves around slowly. But he can shoot backwards with astonishing speed by forcing a steady stream of water through a funnel in his mantle, or shell. This is really jet propulsion with water instead of air or gasses.

Two of the squid's tentacles are much longer than the others. Sometimes each of them can reach out for nearly thirty feet. Their job is to catch living food and pull it in to where the eight shorter and thicker arms

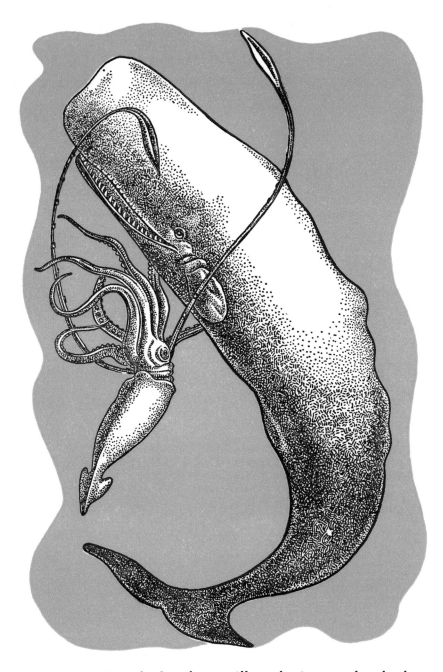

The giant squid, eight feet long, will not hesitate to battle the
sperm whale that may be sixty feet long.

can reach it. When one or more of the short arms get a grip, they carry the victim to the creature's waiting mouth.

There are dozens of different kinds of squids. All of them are much smaller than the giant. Many are called cuttlefish because they have a peculiar sort of lime shell inside their bodies. Pieces of this shell are used to feed canaries and other cage birds.

There is also a peculiar inside gadget called an ink sac. This contains a black liquid named *sepia*. We use this sepia in making watercolor paints. But the cuttlefish has a better idea for it. When thoroughly frightened, he turns on his jet propulsion and darts backward. And at the same time he squirts out some ink which immediately makes a cloud in the water and hides him.

The giant squid has other close cousins called octopuses. They are smaller and have only eight tentacles, which are all the same length. The underside of each one has two rows of suction discs. The body of an octopus is short and baggy. The eyes are very large, and the mouth below them is hideous. It has two great black teeth that look something like a parrot's beak.

The largest known octopus measures up to twenty-

Under the tentacles of an octopus are rows of suction discs.

five feet between the tips of its widespread arms. You have probably read stories about its dragging men out of boats and eating them. Maybe it is strong enough to do this, but I doubt if such a thing ever really happened. The beast's natural habit is to hide among rocks on the ocean bottom and pull in wandering fish and other unsuspecting sea creatures.

Offshore ocean waters in many parts of the world hold another large but entirely different-looking animal.

The sword of a swordfish may be as much as three feet long.

This is the swordfish or broadbill. When fully grown, it may be fifteen feet long and weigh more than 1,000 pounds. There is only a single known species, but this one certainly gets around. It is found on both sides of the Atlantic Ocean, in the Pacific from California to Chile, around Hawaii and Japan, and near Australia and

New Guinea. Everywhere it is famous for its strange shape, terrific speed, and amazing method of feeding.

A swordfish is built somewhat like a chunky, old-fashioned submarine. The oddest thing about it is the flat "sword" which is actually a specially braced extension of the upper jaw. A big one's sword may be three feet long and four or five inches wide at the base. Its owner uses it mostly to kill other fish to eat. He will charge like an express train into a lot of mackerel, herring or other kinds of fish that travel in large crowds or schools. As soon as he gets among them, he slashes his sword wildly in all directions to chop them up. Soon there are plenty of raw fish chunks in the water for him to swallow.

Adult swordfishes have no scales anywhere on their bodies, and they are toothless. Usually the color of their smooth skins is a mixture of bronze and silver. Sometimes it is blackish above and almost white below. The round, bright blue eyes are nearly four inches in diameter. They seem startlingly wide awake as they stare at you.

The eggs of this mighty fish are almost too small to see, and they hatch in two or three days! When the baby swordfishes are a week old, they are only an eighth of an inch long, and both jaws are very short. A month or so later they measure nearly four inches from end to end. About one-third of this is in the jaws, which have toothlike points all over them. Their eyes look as if they were about to pop out of their sockets. A row of long spines runs along the back like a fringe. The

Harpooners watch for fins of the swordfish sticking in the air.

tail is fringed too. You cannot see a sign of a fin anywhere. It seems impossible that the next few months will change this odd little character into a four-foot copy of his gigantic parents.

Swordfishes have been a favorite human food for many years. In our part of the world the usual way of catching them for the market is with a long harpoon. The great fish are wary, but on pleasant days they like to sun bathe so close to the ocean surface that their tall *dorsal* (back) fins stick up into the air. This is the kind of day when harpooners have their greatest success.

The oldtime way of spearing swordfish was from a good-sized sailboat. This craft had an extra-long bowsprit with a small platform and semicircular railing, called the pulpit, out at the end. That is where the harpooner stood with his long-shafted weapon. At the boat's masthead there was another platform for the lookout man. His job was to watch for the back fin of a basking swordfish and give the helmsman directions for sailing cautiously toward it.

Sometimes the swordfish woke up and dived out of sight before the harpooner was close enough for a strike. But if everything went well, the story was different. Slowly, quietly, the boat crept closer and closer. Everyone could see the big fin now, but there was no commotion aboard. Out in the pulpit the harpooner raised his lance higher and higher. A few more yards, and suddenly he struck smoothly and with deadly skill. In an instant the fast and furious battle was on.

Desert Oddities

During daylight hours the desert country of our Southwest looks almost entirely deserted. The sun often heats the soil surface to a temperature of 150 degrees. Nearly all of the many creatures which live there are trying to keep cool in shady hiding places. About the only ones that can stand the terrific heat are lizards and the fantastic horned toads. The hotter things are the better they like it!

These funny, flat little fellows are actually lizards, not toads. In spite of their strange shape and spikes, they are perfectly harmless to people. There are several different kinds of them, all looking more or less alike. And they are only a few inches long.

Horned toads eat practically nothing except live insects. They catch these by scurrying this way and that with astonishing speed. They go so fast and match the color of the desert floor so perfectly that they are very hard to see. When one of them gets fairly close to a bug, he snatches it by shooting out a sticky-tipped tongue the way a true toad does.

Although they dash around as if they were scared, these queer little beasts are quite tame. Of course, rough handling will frighten them. Then they stiffen out and pretend to be dead. Some kinds puff themselves up with air, probably trying to frighten you instead. Others just flatten out. And once in a great while a very badly

The horned toad almost matches the color of the desert floor.

scared horned toad will squirt a threadlike jet of blood from each eye for a distance of two feet or more.

The terrible midday heat suits horned toads so well that even the slight coolness of approaching sunset sends them to bed. This does not take them long. First they stick their noses in the sand and plow a little furrow by working themselves forward a few inches. Then they flatten out and start flicking the sand into the air with the rows of little spines along their sides. It looks almost as if they were throwing the sand grains over their backs with tiny shovels. In this way they can bury themselves in next to no time. Occasionally they leave part of their heads exposed. Either way, you simply cannot see them.

True toads lay eggs from which polliwogs, or tadpoles, hatch. But the so-called horned toads do not do that. Instead of being hatched from eggs, their young are born alive. A single female may give birth to as many as two dozen of them at a time. All of these are exact copies of their mother, spines and all. The only difference is their much smaller size.

The horned toad is an example of a creature that has become adapted to a very special and rugged kind of environment. It would die in some other place which to us would seem to provide an easier life. The desert country is full of these strange lizards.

After dark the gila monster comes out for food on the desert.

In much of the horned toads' territory there is a larger and uglier lizard called the gila (pronounced *hee-la*) monster. It is heavy, fat-tailed, poisonous and as much as two feet long. All over its blackish, pink and yellow skin there are little bumps known as *tubercles*. These look like beads. For this reason scientists list the gila monster as one of the beaded lizards. Quite a number of other species have the same sort of tubercles.

Gila monsters hate the hot sunlight as much as horned

toads enjoy it. All day they hide under rocks or in holes which they dig in the floor of the desert. The bottoms of these holes are well below the surface. The temperature in them is as low as 60 degrees even on the hottest day.

After dark, when everything in the desert is much cooler, the gilas come out and start looking for food. Slowly, steadily they crawl this way and that, poking into holes and crevices for anything good to eat. Not much is known about their special foods. Bird eggs and small rodents such as desert mice are certainly on the menu. Quite likely, too, they gobble large insects and maybe other lizards and small snakes. Whatever the victim may be, it is seized with a quick, strong snap of the powerful jaws.

A gila monster's poison comes from glands located in his lower jaw between the lips and the teeth. There are no hollow fangs to carry it into an opponent's flesh in the manner of rattlesnakes and other pit vipers. Instead, the gila monster has a very special method of his own to put his venom to work. When he gets a good grip on a large enemy, he throws his heavy body from side to side. This thrashing tears the wound larger and larger. At the same time the poison oozing out of the glands follows numerous small grooves in the lizard's teeth. Some of it is pretty sure of getting into the other fellow's bloodstream where it can begin working.

Gila monsters are mean tempered as well as mean looking. When tormented, they will hiss sharply and snap like angry dogs. Anyone who bothers them too much may get into serious trouble.

These frightful, crawling beasts lay about a dozen eggs in a nest several inches underground. The nest is carefully covered with sand or soil to conceal it. The warmth and moisture of the sand hatches the eggs after a while, and the young gilas work their way to the surface. Many other reptiles, such as the snapping turtle, use the same system.

And here is another surprising gila trick. If necessary, this desert dweller can live for several months without eating a thing. All it needs to do is absorb the fat which was stored up in its tail while food was plentiful. This fat is what makes the tail so thick and heavy most of the time. At the end of a really long starvation period, its tail end is so thin that you would hardly recognize it.

3

Toward
the North and
South Poles

The regions around the North and South Poles are different from every other part of the earth. For hundreds of miles in all directions there are no trees. Endless stretches of ice and snow take the place of our open plains and lakes. During the short summer seasons the sun never fully sets. In the long, long winters it never rises. Summer comes to the Arctic (the northern polar country) at the same time of year that it comes to us. But down toward the South Pole, or Antarctic, it is the other way around. The Antarctic has winter when we have summer, and it is summer down there while we are in the middle of winter.

Toward the North and South Poles

Neither the Arctic nor the Antarctic has nearly as many kinds of wild creatures as we do. This is partly because there is less variety in the environments and natural foods. But the beasts that do live toward the two poles are among the strangest ones on earth. Take the arctic walrus, for instance.

An old Pacific bull walrus may be fourteen feet long and weigh close to 3,000 pounds. The distance around him at the shoulders may equal his entire length. Five hundred pounds of fat, or blubber, are spread under his wrinkled, unbelievably tough hide. His two great tusks, or curved teeth, sometimes project two feet or more below his broad, bristly muzzle.

Without these hard ivory tusks, a walrus could not live long. He uses them to dig his favorite meals of clams and other shellfish from the bottom of the ocean. Also they make valuable hooks to help him climb aboard floating ice floes or among big boulders on shore. In fights with other walruses, or perhaps a hungry polar bear that tries to attack him, these tusks are first-class weapons. Chewing is about the only thing he cannot do with them.

Fossil remains show that walruses lived in the United States, England, Belgium and France more than 100,-000,000 years ago. Later, during the Ice Age, they

The great bull walrus will use his ivory tusks to dig shellfish or
to help him climb aboard an ice floe.

ranged down our Atlantic coast as far as South Carolina. A few of them probably existed along the New England shore until the year 1550.

Today the range of the walrus is only from Greenland, Labrador and upper Canada northward as far as the Eskimos and other hardy people have gone. Yet they still follow their age-old habit of living in small herds. The roars and bellows from these tribal groups can be heard as much as a mile away. And how the old bulls do snort through their noses to frighten away an enemy!

Even the biggest and toughest mammal is gentle and devoted at times. So it is not surprising that a mother walrus swims around with her single baby riding comfortably on the back of her neck. He is perfectly safe and satisfied there because he holds on tight with his own small flippers.

The desolate, fog-swept Pribilof Islands lie in the Bering Sea, farther south than the walrus country. They are the home grounds of the famous Alaskan fur seals. These and the walruses belong to the same general group, called *Pinnipeds*. That name comes from two Latin words meaning "fin" and "foot." It fits them well, because their flippers look more like fins than feet.

All About Strange Beasts of the Present

Each year, in May and June, the fur seals swim in from the ocean to breed on these islands. Their pups are born here too. When on shore the seals gather in huge, noisy herds. Every summer there are about 1,500,000 of them altogether. There used to be many more before hunters began slaughtering them for their valuable fur. Today they are protected by strict laws which limit the number that may be killed.

From fall to spring Alaskan fur seals never touch dry land.

Even the largest male fur seals are much smaller than old walruses. But they are not pygmies by any means. They may be six feet long and four feet tall when they raise themselves on their front flippers. Their dense, beautiful fur is blackish on top, reddish underneath, and gray on the shoulders and chest. When they open their mouths to utter harsh, choking roars, you can see the lower canine teeth which make such terrible wounds during their battles with each other.

Each full-grown bull is called a *beachmaster*. He is the boss of a herd or harem of forty to more than 100 females. Most of the savage fights between the beachmasters develop because one of them has tried to steal some females from another fellow.

The cows are mild, gentle creatures a good deal smaller than their mates. Whenever they get hungry, they swim out into the sea and catch fish. But the beachmasters stay on shore for two or three months without eating anything at all. During all this time they live on the fat which is stored in a huge hump on the backs of their necks. It is this fat which gives the forward part of their bodies such a monstrous shape.

A fur seal pup is cute and black and bleats like a lamb. He does not know instinctively how to swim, and his mother gives him no regular lessons. He has to learn by himself, the hard way. At first he just plays around on the beach or rocks at the edge of the water. After a while he plucks up enough courage to get wet and then go in a little way. He will keep on trying even though the waves tumble him around. And a few weeks later he will be almost as good a swimmer as his parents.

By autumn nearly all of the seals have gone back to the sea. From then until the following spring they will not touch a flipper to dry land anywhere. Their journeys will cover many thousands of miles in the North Pacific as far down as California. But when next spring comes, all of them who have escaped such ocean enemies as the killer whale will head again for the good old Pribilofs.

The Far North has some remarkable land mammals too. One of the strangest of these is the muskox. A hundred years ago these chunky, long-haired cattle were probably common in most of arctic America and northeast Greenland. The chances are that there were hundreds of thousands of them. Today there are no more than 20,000. This tremendous drop was caused mostly by men who hunted them with modern rifles.

With lowered heads and great curved horns, muskoxen try to
battle the wolves that attack them.

All About Strange Beasts of the Present

The muskox could often escape primitive bows and arrows. But long-range rifles are too much for him. The instinct of muskox herds is to stand and fight when attacked, instead of running away. So it is easy to shoot them down with bullets.

Wolves are the muskox's worst enemies outside of men with rifles. When a pack of them attacks a herd, the old bulls immediately form a tight circle around the cows and calves. With their lowered heads and great curved horns facing outward, they try to kill every wolf that comes within reach. A few of the cows sometimes join the fighting line. This makes the defense still stronger.

The number of muskoxen in each herd varies from eight or ten to forty or more. These groups wander widely over the treeless tundra of northern Canada, looking for food. They live mostly on grass, tender shoots of dwarf willows and other shrubs, and any flowering plants they can find. Perhaps they also eat moss and even *lichens* (pronounced *lie-kens*), some of which look rather like moss. Sometimes their wanderings take them within 500 miles of the North Pole.

In winter every scrap of vegetation in the Far North is buried under snow. All the fresh water is icebound. But muskoxen do not mind this too much. Instead of drinking water, they eat snow. By pawing and scraping with their big hoofs, they uncover enough vegetation to keep them going. As for the terrible cold, their astonishingly long, thick, brownish winter coats hang almost to the ground and help keep them warm.

During the summer breeding season, the bulls fight savagely by crashing into each other head-on. Often these charges start from a distance of fifty feet. A muskox can run really fast, in spite of his clumsy appearance. So you can imagine the smash when the two battlers meet at full speed.

A bull muskox's tail is only a few inches long, although he measures almost seven feet from end to end. The top of his humped back is four or five feet above the ground, and he weighs more than 500 pounds. His ears are much smaller than those of many other members of the ox family, such as domestic cattle, goats and sheep. But his round eyes are big and remind you a little of a cow's.

Yes, the muskox is quite an animal. Otherwise he could not long survive the fearful hardships of his arctic home.

In many ways the climate and general character of the Antarctic are much like those of the Arctic. The creatures that live there, however, are quite different. You would see no muskoxen, walruses or polar bears if you went to the Antarctic. But you would find penguins. No creature is more astonishing than these tame, almost human-looking birds.

All of the seventeen known penguin species are quite similar in general appearance. They cannot fly at all, partly because their wing feathers are very short. This makes the wings look a good deal like the front flippers of a seal. Under water, however, penguins zip along as fast as fishes. All their swimming strokes are made with the wings. Their strong webbed feet trail out behind and are used only for steering. Sometimes the birds shoot out of the water and down again like porpoises.

On shore these unique birds stand up straight even when they are just waddling around. Their long "arms" hang down at their sides. In their smooth black, white-fronted feather suits they look so much like people that you cannot help laughing.

The emperor penguin is the largest one of all. Dr. Robert Cushman Murphy, a former Director of the American Museum of Natural History and noted expert on the oceanic birds of South America, describes

The egg of the mother penguin (left) rests on her feet and is
kept warm by a blanket of loose, densely feathered skin.

the emperor as being nearly four feet tall and weighing ninety pounds or more. When he is on the huge ice floes, he usually walks bolt upright. But, if he really has to, he can make nine miles an hour by lying on his breast and beating the ice wildly with his feet and wings. By starting deep in the water, he can swim upward so fast that he is able to land upright on an ice floe five feet above the surface.

The emperor's mate, Dr. Murphy says, looks so much like her husband that you cannot tell them apart. She lays her single big egg on the sea ice close to shore. This is done in June, which is the middle of the dark Antarctic winter. The temperature may be 80 degrees below zero, but the mother manages to keep the egg fairly warm without making any nest. First, she places it between her legs and on top of her feet. This keeps it from touching the ice. Then she squats down and covers it with a curious blanket of loose, densely feathered skin which she has for this special purpose. If she has to move somewhere else, she takes the egg along, still resting on the top of her feet. The young penguin will not be ready to hatch for seven or eight weeks. All this time the old lady has to stay on the job!

Dr. Olin S. Pettingill, another well-known ornithologist, has taken marvelous colored movies of penguin life for Walt Disney. This was done near the tip of South America, somewhat to the north of the emperor's home territory. The several species that live there are smaller than the emperors. But all of them are pretty much the same in build, tameness and lively curiosity about new sights.

The mother Adélie penguin is feeding her young.

One of Dr. Pettingill's finest sequences shows a pet penguin following its young mistress out of the house and down the street as happily as if it were a little dog. In another you see a long line of them walking along their ancient trail to the breeding grounds a couple of miles inland. When they come to a little stream trickling down the hillside, they have an awful time trying to hop across it without getting their feet wet. Although they spend much of their lives far out in the salty ocean, they seem to be thoroughly afraid of water that is fresh.

Not all penguin species live in cold regions. One of the smallest kinds, only twenty inches tall, is found as far north as the equator.

Authorities on fossils believe that the history of these peculiar birds goes back at least fifty or sixty million years. In the beginning they may have been able to fly. If so, they probably lost this power after settling in the cold, remote Antarctic where there were not many enemies to attack them.

Nearly all truly antarctic mammals earn their living in salt water. The land areas are so blanketed with snow and ice that there is little for such beasts to eat there. Only the ocean provides enough food to keep them healthy.

Perhaps you wonder how a mammal can get into the sea through ice that often is many feet thick. The explanation lies in the combination of two great world forces—wind and water. Terrific gales are common in antarctic regions. These, battling with the movement of ocean currents, make the surface of the sea restless. Great waves pile up wherever there are large areas of open water. Their powerful heaving swells sometimes travel hundreds of miles. When they come to the fields of polar ice, their force opens cracks here and there. As more swells arrive, the cracks increase in number and size. After a while there are many smaller ice floes instead of a few big ones. In between them there are openings where living creatures can easily get into the water and swim around under the ice.

These water openings have another important value. They make it possible for mammals to come to the surface and breathe. Many species can stay under water for a long time, as the otters and walruses do. But all must come up for air sooner or later. Even the whales, porpoises and other huge mammals have to do this.

Perhaps the fiercest of the aquatic mammals of the Antarctic is the sea leopard. Actually he is a true seal, not a leopard. The last half of his name comes from the round black spots scattered over his coarse, yellowish-gray fur coat. They look a lot like the spots on a leopard.

Sea leopards are from seven to twelve feet long, depending on whether they are males or females. Females are smaller than males, as you would expect. All are powerful, vicious, and have big, strong teeth for grabbing and tearing. They are terrific swimmers too. Otherwise sea leopards could not catch the fish, penguins and other kinds of seals which are among their best-liked foods.

The sea leopard may be from seven to twelve feet long.

All seals like to investigate strange sights. At least one white man learned this in a rather frightening way.

This man, who was an experienced surveyor, had landed on an antarctic ice floe to make some observations. Later, he reported that soon after he set up his instruments a large sea leopard climbed aboard the floe and came toward him. He thought the beast was just being nosy so he shouted and waved his arms to scare it away. Instead of being frightened, the sea leopard bared its teeth, snarled and kept on coming. Then the surveyor carried his equipment farther away. The sea leopard followed, still snarling.

This attack-and-retreat game went on for some time. Finally the sea leopard lost interest and returned to the water. But a few minutes later he stuck his head and shoulders out of the water on the far side of the floe. This time he seemed madder than ever, as if he was daring the man to come into the water and fight it out!

For a long time scientists have wondered how a warm-blooded mammal like the sea leopard can possibly stand the frightful cold of the antarctic air and water. So far they have not found the full answer. When they do, it may be one of the world's most fantastic stories.

4

In
the Tropics
and Subtropics

Beasts of the Land

What is the difference between the tropics and sub-tropics? Well, in general, the tropics are a warm belt that goes completely around the middle of the globe with the equator running through the center. This belt is nearly 25,000 miles long and about 3,400 miles wide. On each side of the belt there is an additional border some 340 miles wide. These two borders are known as the sub-tropics.

Temperatures in the tropics as well as the subtropics depend a good deal on such things as warm or cold ocean currents, directions of prevailing winds, and height above sea level. Some regions are hot and dry, others rainy and perhaps cooler. I have been on South American mountains whose tops are so far above the sea that they are always covered with snow. Yet they are no more than 100 miles from the equator itself.

One of the strangest beasts in the American part of the tropical and subtropical region is the nine-banded armadillo. His native home is Central America, eastern Mexico, and parts of southwestern Texas and nearby states. He has also been introduced into Florida and is doing well there.

A nine-banded armadillo is an animal right out of

Overlapping hoops in the middle permit the armadillo to bend.

the dim, dim past. His head and body together are about fifteen inches long, and so is his tail. From nose to tail tip his upper parts and sides are protected by a suit of armor made of hard, bony plates. Over the shoulders and hips these plates make a solid, immovable sheet. In the middle of the body they are put together in nine overlapping but movable hoops. The tail plates can move too. The result is that the armadillo can bend his tail and the middle part of his body. His legs also can walk and run freely inside the protection of their rigid shields. Young armadillo armor stays soft until the wearer reaches full size. This allows the little fellows to grow up comfortably.

These queer mammals live mostly on ants, various other insects, centipedes, spiders and scorpions. Their teeth do not amount to much. But their long, sticky tongues can sweep up dozens of ants with one lick. Also their strong claws are perfect for uncovering hidden tidbits. An armadillo can dig so fast that he is able to bury himself out of sight in a minute or two. His feet are used, also, for digging an underground burrow six or seven inches wide and many feet long. At the far end, where the leaf and grass nest is, the hole is wider than the entrance door.

A few of the dozen or so armadillo species can roll themselves into completely armored balls when attacked. But the nine-banded armadillo is unable to do this. So when he thinks he is in danger, he either runs for home or digs in wherever he can. He does both of these things with amazing speed.

Today armadillos are found only in the Western Hemisphere. The smallest species is only six inches long. The largest measures three feet, not counting his tail, and weighs nearly 100 pounds. Some of their long extinct ancestors wore absolutely solid armor and were as long as good-sized trucks.

The stretch of land which runs from Mexico to Panama and on into northern South America is truly tropical. Much of it is covered with jungle so dense that sunlight never reaches the ground. For 2,000 miles there are only occasional breaks in the wilderness of lofty trees, slow-flowing streams, and undergrowth so thick that you have to hack your way through it with a swordlike *machete*.

This is the kind of country that tapirs enjoy. They are brownish black, heavy-legged beasts and have practically no tails. Their noses, which extend several inches

The nose of a tapir can move as freely as an elephant's trunk.

beyond their mouths, can move in all directions as freely as an elephant's trunk. Their sense of smell is extremely keen, and they eat all kinds of soft vegetation, including bananas when they can get them. A tapir is a splendid swimmer as well as a fair runner. A fully grown one looks as though he might be a cross between a pig and a small rhinoceros without horns.

He is only about four feet long, but very heavy for his size.

Tapirs are rather shy creatures with poor eyesight. They certainly do not go around looking for trouble. Even so, they often have serious trouble with grim enemies such as jaguars and big constrictor snakes like the boas. When a tapir thinks there is danger around, he heads for the nearest stream at top speed. You can hear him crashing through the jungle like a runaway locomotive. If he wins the race to the bank, he plunges in and swims swiftly away, often beneath the surface. He seems to know that deep water is his best friend. This is one reason why he seldom wanders far away from it.

A tapir prefers to live alone, except during the breeding season. Perhaps this is one reason why he gets along so well. Sometimes he gets up enough courage to raid the gardens of natives living in a jungle clearing. There are even reports that tapirs have been tamed and taught to come when they are called.

The tapir belongs to a group which includes all mammals with hoofs. Each of its feet is made up of *three* hooflike toes, instead of the *two* which deer and cows have. Scientifically, this suggests that tapirs are distant relatives of horses and rhinoceroses. Some scientists think that all three of these mammals are descended from the same ancestors which lived about sixty million years ago. It may be that our modern tapir looks quite like those smaller, long-extinct forebears.

Far back in the past there were tapirs of various kinds almost all over the world. They were common even in the United States. Today, however, there are only four known species of them. Three of these live in Central and South America. The fourth one is in Malaya and Borneo. The reason for the disappearance of all the others is still a first-class mystery.

This tapir is a good example of how peaceful and harmless a tropical jungle beast can be. You certainly could not say that about a coati (pronounced *co-ah-te*). This much smaller mammal is a born scrapper. He will gladly fight almost anything, even his own father and brothers. Such family battles often last until one or the other coati is dead or at least severely wounded.

Coatis are distantly related to raccoons. Their ancestors probably originated some fifteen million years ago. They weigh only fifteen to twenty-five pounds, although occasionally they measure four feet from nose tip to the end of the tail. Nearly half of their total length consists of tail. It is quite a sight to see a coati

Coatis walk with their tails straight up in the air.

walking along a jungle trail with this long tail sticking straight up in the air.

Old male coatis keep pretty much to themselves. But in Central America the females and young travel in bands that may number thirty or forty. These gangs make plenty of noise as they go rummaging through the jungle. They act as if they believe that they can take care of themselves whatever happens. So why bother to keep quiet? Besides, they have good eyesight. This, together with their strong jaws and claws, helps them find and catch many small mammals, young birds, reptiles, spiders, bananas, nuts and berries. As they grunt and scratch and root around, you can hear them for quite a distance. If attacked by a man or some other creature, the old females will defend their youngsters savagely.

Coatis are as much at home in trees as on the ground. They frequently climb to the topmost branches. If these bend under their weight, they don't care a bit. Sometimes the fruit they are after is out of reach. In this case they bend the branch it is on until they can get hold of the tasty food.

A coati's tail is not prehensile so it cannot be curled around a branch like those of some monkeys. But it is perfect for balancing in shaky places. When coatis walk along thin or slippery branches, their tails switch up, down or to one side to help prevent a tumble. They could easily become the world's champion four-footed tightrope walkers.

Coati noses are just as useful as coati tails. There are tough pads on them for protection while rooting in the ground for grubs and other dainties. Much of the food is located by the beast's sense of smell. Finally, he has a funny way of showing anger, pleasure and disgust just by the way he wrinkles up his nose.

These unusual gray-brown raccoon cousins are highly intelligent too. As a rule they do not tame easily. But occasionally one of them gets quite used to being with people. He can be just as amusing and mischievous as a true raccoon. Yet somehow you cannot forget that down inside he is still a wild jungle animal.

A few coatis are to be found in the extreme southern United States close to the Mexican border. This is only because that region, too, is truly tropical.

The coati of the Central American jungles has a somewhat smaller relative that looks a little like him. This is the kinkajou. He is the only American member of the raccoon group that can hang by his tail in the manner of some monkeys. He is definitely a tree dweller so this habit is very useful indeed. There must be many occasions when an extra tail grip comes in handy. Kinkajous range all the way from southern Mexico to southern Brazil. In some places the natives call them night monkeys.

These odd little fellows wear soft coats of yellowish-brown fur. Their heads are broader and rounder than a coati's, and the nose is far shorter. They are much less likely to fight among themselves or with other ani-

Like a monkey, the kinkajou can hang by his tail.

mals. They seem to be perfectly good-tempered as a crowd of them clambers around in the trees, talking back and forth in quiet, chuckling voices.

A kinkajou sleeps in a dark tree hole all day and comes out only at night. Apparently all their feeding is done after dark when they eat almost anything they find among the treetops. You can hear them easily enough through the darkness, but they are almost impossible to see without a good flashlight. When its beam strikes one of them, his big, round, night-seeing eyes show as blazing orange circles.

These curious oddities are often tamed even though they often show bad tempers in captivity. They are always inquisitive and often amusing, but you can never be sure that they will not give you a nip.

A friend of mine kept a kinkajou for nearly a year and never had any trouble with it. He found that it ate many sorts of food besides the meats which, because a kinkajou is carnivorous, would seem to be its favorite meal. My friend taught "Kink" to hang by its tail from his wrist while he walked around a room where cake crumbs had been scattered on the floor. The kinkajou would eat them all up as completely as if he were a vacuum cleaner. Kink never made any real trouble for anybody during his life in civilization. But living in a cold New England house finally became too much for his health. So he had to be turned over to a zoo where the temperature conditions were much better for him.

The tropical forests of the Americas contain many kinds of true monkeys. None of the great apes, such as the gorilla and chimpanzee, are found there. But there are plenty of other strange ones to take their place. Some of them, like the marmosets, are just as interesting and far more attractive.

One marmoset is the world's smallest monkey. It weighs only a few ounces and is less than three inches tall on all fours. Its front feet are paws rather than hands.

A marmoset can scurry through tree branches like a squirrel.

The ends of the toes have claws on them instead of fingernails. Up in the trees where he spends almost all of his time a marmoset scurries around more like a squirrel than a monkey. Also, his voice resembles a bird's chirp so closely that you would never suspect it comes from a monkey's throat.

There are about twenty known species of marmosets. They average eight or nine inches from the nose to the root of the tail. Their tails, however, are longer than the whole head and body. You might expect them to be prehensile so that they could be curled around tree branches for greater safety high in the air. But they absolutely cannot do that.

Marmosets are extremely active, yet seem to have no fear of falling from even the highest, thinnest branch. Apparently they do not mind taking an occasional tumble. There is one record of a marmoset that fell to the ground from a very high branch, landed lightly on its feet, and scampered away as though nothing unusual had happened.

My favorite in this whole tribe of little monkeys is the black-eared marmoset. He measures about eighteen inches from nose tip to tail tip. And more than half of this is in his slender tail. He is very slim, has astonishingly long legs, and his round little face and big eyes look so innocent that you cannot help smiling the minute you see him.

But I think the most remarkable thing about him is the way he is dressed. His soft, fine-haired fur is very dense and close-fitting. The whole tail and the rear half of the body are ringed and barred with black and light gray. His tiny face is brown with a white forehead. And over his shoulders and around his neck there is a broad strip of black which looks for all the world like a woman's old-fashioned winter cape.

The top of this amazing midget's head has a round black patch exactly like a cap. And at the very tip of each small ear there is a tuft of straight black hairs nearly two inches long. Some of these stand straight up, others flare out to the sides. You just cannot imagine the startled expression they give him!

Not even in the mysterious depths of the American tropics would you expect to find a beast that eats and sleeps upside down in trees, is almost blind, and has plants growing in his hair. The very idea of such a creature sounds completely crazy. But it does exist today, and there is plenty of scientific proof that the statements you have just read are true. This creature is called a sloth, which means "laziness." Many thousands of years ago the sloth's ancestors lived on the ground and sometimes were as big as elephants.

The two known living species of sloth are found only in the New World. They look almost exactly alike except that one has three toes on each of its front feet, and the other only two. The three-toed sloth eats hardly anything except the leaves of cecropia trees. The two-toed will eat many kinds of leaves. Nobody seems to know why their meals are different.

A sloth weighs no more than a medium-size dog, although his undercoat of fluffy hair and the long outer hairs make him look quite large. All four legs are amaz-

The sloth walks upside down, going hand-over-hand under a branch.

ingly long, and so are the curiously curved nails which form most of the feet. On the ground he can barely shuffle around. He is a pretty good tree climber, though, as well as a fast swimmer. Where he feels really at home is among the more or less horizontal tree limbs. That is where he lives upside down.

Both kinds of sloths use the same method of moving from place to place in a tree. All four of their permanently curved feet are hooked over the branch. Down below is the body, dangling by its skinny legs. Progress along the branch is made by a slow, hand-over-hand movement. It looks a little like walking upside down if you can imagine such a thing.

A favorite sleeping position is on a horizontal branch directly below another one. The sloth rests his rump on the bottom branch, hooks his feet over the upper branch, curls up, and quietly passes out for the night. There is no danger of falling out of bed because his curved feet cannot straighten out and lose their grip. Nor does he have to bother about what to do with his tail, for he does not have one.

Sloths have the world's dumbest faces. Their small, weak, dull gray-brown eyes show no expression whatever. The brain behind them is as stupid as they are. The only sound the beast ever makes is a soft, wheezy whistle and maybe a faint whimper.

Next to their inverted way of living, perhaps the most incredible thing about sloths is their reddish brown hair. There is plenty of it, and the longest hairs grow along the chest and stomach. If the creatures were to stand up, like other mammals, these long hairs would touch the ground. But in their normal bottom-side-up position, they naturally hang down over the creature's sides so thickly that they make a first-class raincoat on wet days.

In the Tropics and Subtropics

The little plants I spoke of live in this long, dense hair. They are called *algae* (pronounced *al'-gee*), and they have no stems, leaves, flowers or seeds. They are one of the earth's earliest forms of life. Their ancestors appeared perhaps a billion years ago. That was long before even the first of what we now think of as true plants.

These millions of almost microscopic growths are very valuable to a sloth. In wet weather they give his coat a greenish color. When the dry season comes and much of the jungle looks more gray-green, the algae also turn that color. So, in dry times as well as rainy ones, they help to camouflage the sloth so perfectly that you can hardly see him.

These incredible beasts have many dangerous enemies. Perhaps the worst of them are pumas, jaguars and boas, all of which can climb trees. In a hand-to-hand fight, a sloth would not have much of a chance. Its only weapons are those strong, hooklike feet, which it might possibly use with some effect.

You may wonder why such a slow, stupid creature was not wiped out long ago by big foes. There are several reasons. First, sloths move so slowly that they do not attract attention. Also, their algae camouflage makes them extremely hard for even the sharpest eyes to see. Besides these advantages, their bodies hang so far below a tree limb that they are not easy for one of the big cats to reach.

Added to all this, a sloth is very difficult to kill. It has so many more ribs than other mammals that only the strongest foe can crush it. Also, its skin is amazingly tough. Best of all, perhaps, the sloth can be terribly wounded and still keep on living. There is an apparently reliable report of a sloth's heart which continued to beat for half an hour after a surgeon had separated it from the body.

Anteaters are another American tropical tribe that has been around for a long while. About sixty million years ago, early in the Tertiary Period, they were already in existence. At one time there were hundreds of kinds in both North and South America. Today there are only three. The most fabulous of these is certainly the giant anteater.

This largest of his race is six or seven feet overall, although he measures hardly more than two feet high at the shoulders. His neck and head are unbelievably long and so nearly the same thickness that you cannot tell where one ends and the other begins. He has no

The anteater shoots out a sticky, wormlike tongue to catch ants.

teeth at all, and his mouth is a round hole just big enough for him to shoot out a sticky, wormlike tongue for a foot or so. Eyes, nose, ears and brain are absurdly small for a beast of his size. And he is almost as blind as a bat.

An anteater shuffles along somewhat like a bear. But there is this difference between the two mammals: a bear walks on the soles of his feet, while an anteater walks on the outsides of his. His gait is pigeon-toed, with the four-inch claws turned backward along the inside of the feet. This gets them out of the way. Also it saves wear and tear on them. Their owner must keep them sharp so that they can rip open the ant and termite hills from which he gets most of his food.

Next to his peculiar build and gait, perhaps the most fantastic part of a giant anteater is his enormously bushy tail. It is about two feet long, and he often holds it over his back squirrel fashion. Perhaps it helps to keep him warm as well as dry during a rainstorm. Some naturalists think that he also uses it to keep flies away.

This grotesque beast feeds by day as well as by night. He is too slow and clumsy to run away if attacked. But do not think for one moment that he is unable to defend himself. If necessary he will stand up on his hind legs like a bear, with his heavy tail out behind for a balance prop. Then, when the enemy charges, he will swing terribly with those powerful, big-clawed front legs. One good swipe will tear a fair-sized foe to shreds. If this is not enough, the anteater will crush him to death in a bearlike hug.

These gray, black and white anteaters are almost always ground-dwellers. Occasionally, however, they manage to climb trees after the soft parts of bird eggs and young birds. They cannot eat these in the usual way because they have no teeth or regular jaws. But they can crush the small victims and lick up the juice with that astounding tongue which darts in and out like lightning.

The two other anteater species I mentioned are both tree dwellers. They are short-haired and have prehensile tails. The smaller one is squirrel-size, and his coat is a glossy golden color. And the middle-size one is about as big as a slim fox.

The American tropics hold another monstrous beast that is just as famous as the anteater. It is the giant tortoise or land turtle. His natural home is on the harsh, volcanic islands which form a group known as the Galapagos Archipelago. There are about sixty of these islands altogether. A few are quite large, and the others very small. They are located in the Pacific Ocean 500 miles west of Ecuador. The line of the equator runs right through them.

This huge tortoise has a carapace that may be more than four feet long. When an old one stands up, the top of his shell is three feet above the ground. His greatest weight is probably 500 pounds, and the chances

The legs of a Galapagos turtle look like those of an elephant.

are that he can live for 500 years. Scientists think that he may be the longest-lived vertebrate animal in the modern world.

It takes good legs to carry such a mighty beast up hill and down in country that is cluttered with big volcanic rocks. The giant tortoise certainly has such legs. They look more like the legs of an elephant than those of a turtle. The feet are especially elephant-like. When the tortoise travels, he never crawls the way most turtles do. Instead, his lower shell is raised a foot above the ground and his steps are slow, heavy and regular. He can easily carry a full-grown man on his back, if the man can manage to hold on!

It is an astonishing experience to watch one of these tortoises going somewhere. His scrawny neck is quite thin compared with his legs. It sticks out and up for nearly two feet. And at its end is a weird, snaky-looking head that seems to be a thousand years old.

The giant tortoises of the Galapagos live mostly in the higher parts of the islands, perhaps a half mile above sea level. There they find pools of fresh water where they drink enormously during the rainy season. That is the time when they store up water for the dry times which always follow. They also find moisture in their favorite foods, such as grass, berries, flowers, and the leaves of cactus and other kinds of plants.

Long ago there were probably many thousands of these great turtles. But men have slaughtered them so recklessly that they are now quite rare. For centuries the crews of ships that put in to the islands for fresh water have butchered them for their meat. Native hunters camp on the islands to kill them for the sake of the excellent oil which is contained in their fat. Another peril is the numerous wild dogs, descended from domestic ones aboard visiting ships. These animals cannot kill a large tortoise, of course. But they can and do dig up the turtles' 2 1/2-inch eggs and eat them. Even if an egg escapes long enough to hatch, the young tortoise will not be safe from these wild dogs until he is at least a foot long.

These remote islands of the Galapagos group contain many other smaller but equally strange beasts. For example, there is the sea iguana, the only marine lizard in the world today. He is black when wet, gray when dry; and he blows puffs of vapor from his nostrils as if he were a fairy-tale dragon. A big one is nearly four feet long. He and all his companions swim easily without using their legs at all. Their strokes are only wrig-

The sea iguana blows puffs of vapor from his nostrils.

gles of the tail and the rear part of the body. Naturalists call these movements undulations. They look somewhat like the sidewise wriggling of a snake.

Sea iguanas are quite timid, and they lead rather easy lives. Dr. William Beebe, when he studied them in their homeland, found that they spend the night in earth burrows or in deep rock crevices. They get up about eight or nine o'clock in the morning on sunny days. If the tide is high, they lie around waiting for it to go out. Then, at low tide, they go down to the edge of the surf and feed on the short, soft algae which are their special dish. This is their only meal of the day. After it, they go to comfortable rocks or piles of dry seaweed well back from the water's edge and bask there until it is time to go to bed again.

All About Strange Beasts of the Present

These iguanas, Dr. Beebe reported, have excellent eyesight. On the other hand, they seem to be very hard of hearing. Not too much is known about their nesting habits. But we do know that their eggs are white, soft-shelled and about three inches long.

The iguana tribe is a large one. Some of the kinds that live in Central and South America grow to be six feet long. These mainland fellows are mostly jungle beasts. They have fantastic spinelike points on their heads, along the back, and out on the tail. The loose, baggy throat skin, which can be puffed out with air as a defense or offense threat, is one of the oddest things about them. You would be amazed, too, by the flavor of their meat when properly cooked. It tastes a good deal like delicious chicken.

Like some of the other lizard types, land iguanas are surprisingly fast runners. I learned this on a small island in the Bay of Panama where I once spent a week or so. Most of the island was quite high, dry and covered with dense brush and woods. But on the end nearest the mainland there were several buildings in a good-sized clearing.

Every day, in the morning or afternoon, a four-foot iguana used to leave the forest and hunt for food along

The land iguana can tear along as nimbly as a dog.

the open part of the shoreline. From the porch of one of the buildings I could see that he was wary, although he never seemed to be really afraid. He stood right up on all four legs and kept looking this way and that.

One day he went so far down the shore that I thought I would be able to cut him off before he could get back to the safety of the forest. He must have seen me coming, for he turned suddenly and took off for home at top speed. I ran, too, planning to head him off. But I was much too slow for that. He made it into the woods with yards to spare, tearing along as nimbly as a dog.

Was he badly scared? No, I don't think so. You see, he and I had several more such races before I left the island. And he won all of them easily!

All About Strange Beasts of the Present

For hundreds of years travelers in the jungles of the New World have told tales of huge, frightful bats which sucked the blood of human beings and sometimes killed them. No particular name was given to these monsters in the beginning. But as the reports spread, people began calling them vampire bats because they were said to behave as European vampires were believed to do. A real vampire, you know, is supposed to be a fiendish ghost that comes out of a human grave at night and kills the dead person's enemy by sucking out all his blood. Of course, there never were such creatures and never will be. Vampires are just an old superstition that exists only in the imaginations of foolish people.

Like many other weird reports from remote parts of the world, there was a grain of truth in those early stories of vampire bats. Actually there are at least three species of bats which live on the blood of other warm-blooded animals. But all of them are small and not nearly so wild-looking as some of the insect-eating kinds. As far as we know, they are found only in the American tropics. Also, they never suck blood from their victims. Their method is to lap it up with their tongues. Their stomachs cannot hold much so many

Vampire bats live on the blood of other warm-blooded animals.

attacks would have to be made on a person before his loss of blood could become serious.

Vampire bats fly only at night. If one of them gets into a tent or a room where a person is sleeping, he may try for a meal. Without making a sound, he starts looking for an uncovered foot, arm, hand, nose or some other part of the body. When he finds one, he settles on it so gently that not even the lightest sleeper would wake up. Then, with his razor-sharp front teeth, the vampire swiftly cuts a round hole in the skin. It is only about an eighth of an inch in diameter and half as deep, but immediately it starts to bleed very freely. During the next eight or ten minutes the bat laps up a full meal with his specially shaped tongue. Then he flies away as quietly as he came. Usually the sleeper knows nothing about it until he wakes up in the morning and finds himself smeared with blood.

You would think that the pain of receiving such a wound would awaken anybody quickly. No one seems to know just how the bat prevents this. Some scientists think that he may apply some kind of pain-killing liquid from inside his mouth. Possibly there is also something that keeps the blood from thickening, or clotting, when it reaches the air. Anyway, there is not the least doubt about these two facts: First, cutting the hole causes no pain. And second, the blood continues flowing for an unusually long time.

Vampire bat damage is most dangerous to the little wild mammals, and perhaps some birds, whose entire supply of blood is so small that they cannot afford to lose any of it. However, cattle, mules, horses and some other big animals are sometimes badly weakened by many attacks repeated night after night. It is also sus-pected that these bats carry a serious cattle disease from one animal to another.

In the Old World

Although vampire bats are literally bloodthirsty, they measure only about four inches in length and perhaps

Fruit-eating bats sleep upside down during the daytime.

one foot from tip to tip of their outspread wings. This is very small compared with their fruit-eating cousins in the Old World. Some of these big fellows have a wingspread of four or five feet. Their common name of flying foxes fits them well. They have foxlike ears, eyes and long muzzles; and their fur is mostly brown and blackish. Even their bodies are about the size of small foxes.

Members of this fruit-eating branch of the bat family are found in many warm parts of the Old World. They are especially common in southern Asia and the islands of the South Pacific. They are far from being savage creatures and seem to be so sociable that they sleep in colonies that may number several thousand. It is an astonishing experience to pay a daytime visit to one of these community dormitories. You will see many tree limbs thickly festooned with sleeping fruit-eaters hanging by their hind feet. In this strange upside-down position, with their long wings folded around them, they remind you of a terrific crop of huge brown pears.

I have never heard of fruit bats being harmful to man or beast. The worst thing that can be said about them is that they sometimes damage valuable fruit crops. In places where they are particularly numerous the fruit growers may have to place nets over their trees to protect the ripening crop.

In general, bats are the only known mammals that can truly fly. There are more than 450 species of them, ranging in size from these flying foxes down to midgets smaller than mice. Although their thin, leathery wings have no feathers, they can fly better than most birds. On the ground they can do little more than flop around. Their very lives depend upon their fantastic skill in the air.

The hyena and the jackal (left) feast on decaying flesh.

The tropical and subtropical parts of Africa, Syria, Mesopotamia and India are famous for their numbers of strange beasts far larger than the flying foxes. Many of these are more amusing than dangerous. But there are a few kinds, such as the hyenas, that really deserve to be called horrid.

There are three species of hyena—the striped, the spotted and the brown. All of them are as big as large, fierce, very heavily built dogs. Their tails are short and bushy at the end. The necks, heads and jaws are extremely powerful, even for animals of this size. Another peculiar fact is that their shoulders are considerably higher than their hindquarters. This forward height is still more noticeable because of the coarse, bristly hair which covers the neck as well as the shoulders. The general color is a dirty brown with blackish spots or stripes according to the species.

All three kinds of hyenas are meat eaters. But they do not care whether the meat is fresh or so old that it smells bad. Wherever they go, they are known as scavengers, which means that they will gobble up just about any worthless, discarded flesh that they can find. They are very likely to hang around hunters' camps, attracted by the smell of meat that has been thrown away. Often, too, they sneak into the edges of native villages for the same purpose.

Most of a hyena's scavenging is done at night after he has slept all day in some cave or other dark retreat. If food is scarce, he usually hunts alone and may travel long distances. On the other hand, whole packs of hyenas quickly assemble at the body of a dead horse or other big animal. Such a discovery promises a real meal for any creature strong enough to get it. And these unpleasant scavengers certainly are strong!

Hyenas utter a variety of snarls, howls and other repulsive sounds. The striped species, which is found in northern Africa and northeastward to India, has an especially frightening voice. He is often called the laughing hyena because one of his calls sounds somewhat like horrible human laughter.

While I was working on this book, I came across an old official British Government report on the damage done by wild beasts in India during the year 1878. An especially interesting part of it was about these same striped laughing hyenas. It showed that in this particular year they had killed thirty-three people. Their record for 1877 was twenty-four people killed. So it looks as though they are even more ferocious than most of us think.

The true chameleon of Asia Minor and the Mediterranean Sea region is startlingly different from those grim hyenas. He is a harmless little fellow in spite of his fabulous appearance. And some of the things he can do are even more amazing than his crested head and long, prehensile tail.

With the flash of his tongue the chameleon snags an insect.

Perhaps the most remarkable thing about this lizard is his ability to change the color of his rough but scale-less skin. Normally he is gray-green with dark spots except for some pale brown on his sides. In darkness, though, he quickly fades to a pale cream color speckled with yellow. Put him out in the hot sun, and you will see him change to a dull black all over. High temperature without sunlight makes his skin green. And in cool, shaded places he is a dull gray.

A chameleon's feelings also produce color changes. Thus, excitement and fear make him turn pale. But when he gets mad, he switches back to dark colors!

All of these color variations are under the perfect

control of the chameleon's nervous system. The machinery which actually produces them is absolutely incredible.

In the first place, the outer layer of skin is transparent. Just under it there is a layer of tiny cells or pockets. Some of these hold a white substance. Others are filled with yellow. Beneath this second layer there is a third one containing larger black and red cells.

When the chameleon becomes very excited, a set of very thin threads or filaments, filled with a blotting-out substance, spreads a sort of curtain around and over the layer of light-colored cells. This makes the skin of the little lizard turn dark. The same thing happens when the temperature or light conditions call for dark clothes. And when it is time to turn light, the curtain is withdrawn, and the light cells show again.

Among the muscles just under the skin, there is also a set of special air cells. These are connected with the chameleon's extremely large lungs. So, whenever he feels like it, he can blow himself up until he looks almost like a toy balloon.

Chameleons spend practically all their time among the branches of trees and large bushes. There they crawl about very slowly, holding on with all four "hands" and often with their tails. Their necks are so short that they can hardly turn their heads. But their big, pop eyes can roll in all directions independently of each other. It is no trick at all for a chameleon to look behind him with one eye and ahead with the other.

Each eye is protected by a tough membrane, or skin, which has a peephole in the center directly over the pupil of the eye. This membrane moves with the eye so that the chameleon can always see perfectly.

When a chameleon creeps within range of a nice juicy insect, his amazingly long tongue darts out like a flash. Its sticky tip snags the bug and snatches it back into the hunter's open mouth. Then there is a satisfied gulp, and that is that. The whole action, except for the gulp, has been so swift that you could scarcely see what happened.

Along the mountainous border of southwestern China, away to the east of chameleon territory, is the land of the world-famous giant panda. He is built rather like a smallish, extra-fat bear; but his friendly, almost jolly face is unlike that of any bear that ever lived. As a matter of fact, he is not a bear at all. Authorities believe that he is distantly related to the coati and kinkajou of

Even in winter the giant panda feasts on bamboo shoots.

the American tropics as well as to our own amusing raccoon.

Although this panda lives in the subtropical belt, his part of China is so mountainous and so far inland from the South China Sea that snow falls every winter. This does not bother old funny-face in the least. Perhaps a bear might go into hibernation when the flakes begin to fall, but not the giant panda. His mountains are heavily forested with bamboo. The tender shoots and leaves of this peculiar plant are his principal food. The result is that he is perfectly satisfied to spend the winter wandering around and munching bamboo whenever he feels like it.

This king-size teddy bear is clownish in markings as well as movements. The whole head and neck are white except for a black nose tip, ears, and a ring around each eye. The black of the front legs continues up and over the shoulders as if it were a strap holding up his trousers. Then comes more white extending backward to his stump of a tail. Only the lower part of the hind legs is black.

Probably the giant panda was never really common, even in its remote mountain home. It is quite rare today, partly because its astonishing appearance and strange ways have attracted hunters from all over the world. Occasionally one is captured alive and sent to a zoo. That is about the only chance most of us have to see it except in pictures or as a mounted specimen in a large museum.

These Choose the Water

Returning now to the American tropics, you could not ask for a more frightful beast than the crocodile. It belongs to a group of aquatic reptiles that are known around the world for their great size, terrific jaws and slashing, armor-plated tails. Our New World species reaches a length of about fourteen feet. His largest relative lives in Madagascar and may be thirty feet long.

The sides and belly of an American crocodile are covered with scales that look and feel like very hard leather. His whole back wears an armor of many bone-like plates anchored firmly in the under skin. Some people think that these give him complete protection against rifle bullets. This is not really true. Bullets and even arrows can get through. But the plates certainly are a good defense against wild animal enemies.

Besides their amazing length and rows of wicked teeth, a crocodile's jaws are noted for something that

The crocodile is at home on land and in the water. He swims
fast or slowly by swinging his tail from side to side.

cannot be seen. They can close with such power that they may clip off a person's arm or leg with one snap. Yet a man with strong hands can grab a crocodile's snout and keep the mouth from *opening* at all.

A crocodile's color varies from yellowish brown to nearly black. You usually find the lighter colors where the water is clear. This is because they make good camouflage under such conditions. The blackish color hides him better in muddy water.

These appalling beasts have several ways of catching their prey. One is to lie motionless in a marsh or shallow water with only their protruding eyes and nostrils above the surface. At such times they look for all the world like old dead tree trunks with two or three branch stubs sticking up. Any creature foolish enough to step on such a "log" may never have a chance to do it again!

Another favorite method used by crocodiles might be called the rush-and-grab attack. This is aimed at animals careless enough to stand on a low bank next to fairly shallow water. If a crocodile is near by, he will simply charge ashore with astonishing speed, seize his prey and plunge back into the water with it. He can eat just as well under water as on land. The water will not get into his ears, because they are fitted with flaps which can be closed tight whenever he needs them. Crocodiles kill many native children in this way every year.

A crocodile is an expert swimmer at fast as well as very slow speeds. He swims entirely by swinging his mighty tail from side to side. His fellow reptile, the sea iguana, has a similar stroke. The tail is also used to hit terrific sidewise blows for either offense or defense. Although these may not always cripple or kill the other fellow, they often throw him within reach of those terrible jaws. Finally, when an old bull crocodile gets really upset, he lets out a sudden roar like the end of the lion's famous challenge.

Crocodiles are found in salt water as well as fresh water from Florida to Mexico and southward through Central America and the West Indies to Venezuela, Colómbia and Ecuador. They look much like alligators.

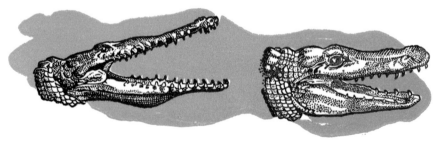

A crocodile's snout (left) is more pointed than an alligator's.

In the Tropics and Subtropics

You can tell these two great reptiles apart by their heads. A crocodile has a long, pointed snout. The alligator's snout is a good deal broader. Alligators, by the way, are sometimes found as far north as southern North Carolina.

Many of the fresh-water streams in Brazil, the Guianas and the Amazon River country east of the Andes Mountains contain aquatic beasts far stranger than any crocodile. They are called electric eels because they are loaded with live electricity. Touch one of them just once, and he will give you a shock that you will never forget!

These remarkable creatures are not true eels, although they look much like them. They average about three feet long. Sometimes they reach a length of seven feet and a thickness of six inches or so. The general effect is of a scaleless, almost round snake with a ribbon-like fin along his belly from the head to nearly the tip of the tail. The color may be olive-green, greenish black, blue-gray or reddish.

Four-fifths of an electric eel's body is filled with organs which generate and store the electricity. His stomach and all his other life organs are crowded into his front end.

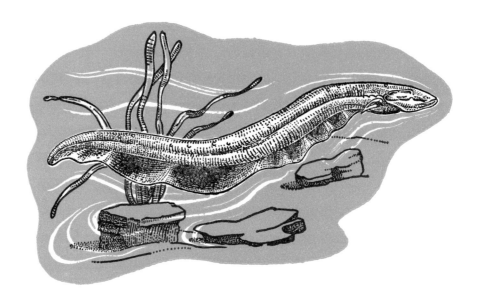

An electric eel can give a shock of 300 to 500 volts.

This incredible creature has three pairs of electricity producers. Each one is equipped with plates which operate like those in a car's storage battery. In a seven-foot specimen the biggest pair is five feet long and has thirty to thirty-six plates. The middle-sized pair, nearly as long but thinner, contains fourteen to twenty plates. There are still fewer plates in the shortest pair, which extends from the middle of the body to the end of the tail.

The electric eel has full control over the kind of shock he gives out. The lightest ones probably come from his smallest batteries. Some authorities think these are used to warn other fish to keep away. The chances are that the middle-sized pair produces the 30- to 40-volt jolts. These would be for what you might call everyday food-catching use. And finally, there are the real blockbusters of 300 to 500 volts from the largest batteries. This is two or three times the voltage used in an ordinary house. A single such shock can give a severe jolt to an enemy as large as a man or even a horse. The big victim usually recovers after a time. But there is always the possibility that he will be killed. Smaller creatures probably never know what hit them.

Merely touching an electric eel will give you one of these severe shocks. No "live" electric wire could jar you more swiftly.

One of the oddest facts about this impossible beast is that its electricity may have been put to some human use. For a long time certain tribes of South American Indians have treated cases of rheumatism with electric eel shocks! They believe that shocks of the right strength help the patient get well. Perhaps they do. After all, our own doctors use electric treatments for some diseases, don't they?

These eels and a few other fishes are the only animals known to produce electricity. All of them have thin skins, move slowly, and prefer shallow water. One kind is the torpedo ray, found in the Atlantic and Pacific Oceans as well as the Mediterranean Sea. There is also a fresh-water electric catfish in the Nile River. And here in America we have a strange little character, known as the stargazer, that carries his own storage batteries with him.

The next to largest seal species in the world lives in salt water along the southern coast of North America. He cannot boast of being able to make his own electricity. But he does have the saddest eyes and the strangest way of swimming you ever saw. He is the northern elephant seal, and he sometimes measures seventeen feet long and weighs over 5,000 pounds.

Elephant seals have no ears, and their rear flippers cannot be moved forward. In the water, however, these hind flippers work like twin boat propellers and push the big fellow ahead at moderate speed. Meanwhile his front flippers are held against his sides and do nothing at all. Apparently they just go along for the ride. In this strange fashion he manages to catch enough slow-swimming fish and bunches of seaweed to keep his stomach pretty well filled.

An elephant seal moves still more slowly when he

When frightened, the elephant seal can inflate his muzzle.

lands on some beach or rocky island. His great weight makes it impossible for him to flop ahead in the manner of most seals. So he uses a system that is entirely his own. Massive ripples flow through his body from bow to stern and gradually push him forward. This peculiar performance suggests the crawling of a gigantic caterpillar.

The "elephant" part of this strange monster's name comes from the trunklike snout which projects beyond the male's muzzle. This trunk usually hangs limp and almost falls into his mouth when he barks. But when he gets excited, or wants to frighten an enemy, he inflates it with air until his head looks like the homeliest of Halloween masks.

Another of the elephant seal's oddities is its habit of shedding its yellowish brown skin twice a year. The hide does not come off in one piece as a snake's skin does. Its owner gets rid of it a little at a time, more or less the way a person's skin peels after a bad sunburn. Some of the frayed old pieces are larger than your hand.

Sixty or seventy years ago there were probably not more than 100 of these giant, rather helpless beasts in existence. All the rest had been killed by commercial hunters. Then the Mexican government passed strict protection laws to save them from complete extinction. Today there are more than 6,000 of them, and their number is increasing every year.

The largest of all seals is the southern elephant seal. This form is almost exactly like the northern species except in size. The bulls are known to reach a length of twenty feet and a weight of more than three tons. Their home is in the Antarctic and sub-antarctic.

The oceans of the world contain countless creatures so primitive that they would have felt completely at home in prehistoric days. Nowhere else on the globe, perhaps, are there so many strange beasts that have changed so little through millions of years.

One important reason for their being alive today is that their environment is practically the same as it was ages and ages ago. Another is that enormous areas of the sea are still undisturbed by mankind. To be sure, ships steam along the surface and wartime depth charges have been dropped into the sea. Submarines and divers sometimes explore its depths for considerable distances. But, in general, modern life has affected it very little. It still remains our greatest natural wonderland.

The manta is a good example of this existence of the past in the present. In one form or another this spectacular beast is found in the tropical and subtropical parts of all the oceans and of the Mediterranean Sea. The species which you meet in this book lives in American Atlantic as well as Pacific waters. On the Atlantic side it has been known to wander as far north as New Jersey. Along our western coast its range meets that of the elephant seal.

Mantas are dark brownish above and whitish underneath. Instead of regular fins they have broad, somewhat pointed "wings" with which they flap through the water more or less as a bird flies through the air. A long, whiplike tail trails out behind. A fully grown manta, or devil ray, may be 20 feet wide from tip to tip and weigh more than 3,000 pounds.

The manta's head is just as astonishing as its body. The neckless head is quite flat on top and very broad. At the outer edge, on each side, there is a fair-sized eye. Just forward of each eye there is a peculiar "clasper" which sticks out in front like a spiral when the beast is swimming. These two claspers or "cephalic fins" can bend quickly in any direction. The manta uses them to scoop fairly small fish into its wide, underneath mouth. The mouth itself also gulps in plankton and other very small creatures.

Apparently these odd claspers instinctively close on almost anything that gets between them. Suppose, for instance, that the manta swims head-on into the cable of an anchored small boat. More often than not his claspers will grab it and hang on. The next thing you know the manta charges ahead, yanks up the anchor, and takes boat and all on the wildest kind of ocean ride. Boatmen who have had such an experience never want to repeat it!

The manta can hurl itself through the air in strange fashion.

Other kind of rays, including the common "skates" which you may have seen along our beaches in summer, lay eggs. But no manta ever laid an egg in its life. Instead, its young are born alive. This is only one of its peculiarities for which scientists have not yet found the full answer.

Another mystery is the manta's habit of hurling itself high into the air and falling back to the water with a tremendous splash that can be heard far away. Several times, off the northwest coast of South America, I have seen four or five of these monsters put on their peculiar air show one after the other. Some scientists think the mantas may do it to get rid of annoying parasites clinging to their skins. John T. Nichols, a prominent fish specialist at the American Museum of Natural History, tells me that he thinks they make their spectacular jumps just for fun. Whatever the reason may be, everybody agrees that it is one of the most astonishing sights in the world.

Every once in a while a salt-water fisherman in the West Indies or along the Florida coast lifts his net and finds in it a small creature that seems to be neither fish, flesh nor fowl. It is only a foot long or even less. Its flattened, warty, grayish-brown body is quite heart-

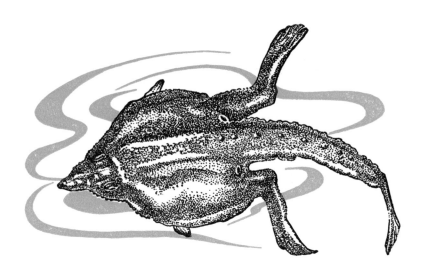

Apparently the batfish walks on the bottom instead of swimming.

shaped when seen from above. Sticking out behind there is a somewhat fishlike tail that has a little fin on top and another one below. A sword-shaped snout reaches forward from between two cold-looking eyes. Below the base of the snout there is a small, grim mouth.

The fisherman's first glimpse of the beast may be when it climbs the side of the net with two pairs of impossible legs, looks around, and quickly ducks back into the water. Usually he has no idea that he has just been looking at one of the batfishes.

The batfish breaks all the rules of what a fish should be. Apparently it walks on the bottom instead of swimming through the water. Yet its so-called legs are believed to be modified fins. Little or nothing is known about its foods, general habits or ancestors. It does have a few living relatives that look a good deal like it except for their shorter snouts. On the other hand, it is not at all uncommon in rather shallow salt water. In summer it occasionally shows up as far north as southern New England.

Batfishes are believed to move around by means of their two pairs of modified fins. The forward ones are short and perhaps serve the purpose of arms. The rear ones are jointed in such a way that they can take quite long strides. At the end of each hind leg, where you might expect to find a foot, there is only a finlike web.

No one knows how many species of batfish actually exist. Now and then a new one shows up somewhere. Only a few years ago such a species was caught by a fisherman among the Galapagos Islands. As I write this, the scientists have not decided on a suitable name for it. Its snout is considerably shorter than that you have just read about. Just below this snout, but above the actual mouth, there is a sizable hole in which there are two peculiar yellowish objects. These are attached to a sort of stem. It is believed that the batfish waves them around in the water to attract living food close enough for him to grab and eat.

5

In the
South Pacific

Ground and Tree Dwellers

Parts of the great island group which we call the South Pacific Islands are endlessly exciting because of their unbelievable wild animals. So many peculiar ones live there today that you feel as though you were in a different world. New Guinea, Australia and New Zealand are especially interesting to people who like to look back over the long trail that connects our present days with those of the vanished past.

Take the flightless, chicken-size kiwi of New Zealand, for instance. Its long, loose, blackish feathers look almost like hair. It has neither wings nor tail. Its slender, curved, straw-colored bill is about six inches long and is perfectly suited for picking up stray bits of food on the ground. The only way the bird can get around is by walking. So, after countless centuries of life on foot, its legs and feet are amazingly large and strong. For another oddity, the males do all the work of building the nest, incubating the eggs and caring for the kiwi chicks. All the females have to do is lay the eggs.

And then there are the next-to-impossible cassowaries. Three species of them are found in the Bismarck Archipelago and northern Australia. All of them have enormous three-toed feet and powerful legs, but they cannot fly at all. There are no regular flight feathers on their very small wings. The place of such feathers on each wing is taken by a set of stiff, springy spikes, somewhat like the tines of a pitchfork. These are used to push aside branches and other obstructions when the bird runs through dense jungle. It may travel as fast as thirty miles an hour in such places. Besides the tines, the cassowary has a fantastic black, bony growth on top of its head. This serves as a "crash helmet" in case its wearer hits anything head-on.

A cassowary is nearly five feet tall when it stands

The cassowary can walk and swim, but cannot fly at all.

up straight. Its glossy black plumage is thick and loose like the kiwi's. The gawky, almost featherless neck and head are blue, red and purplish. Its voice is a great booming croak. And the huge eggs it lays are green, rough-shelled, and as hard as ivory.

There are no webs between the cassowary's thick toes. However, he is an excellent swimmer. He plows across a broad river with his body submerged and only his snaky neck and head visible above the surface. If he finds himself near the ocean shore, he may wade out through the surf and swim around, apparently just for fun.

Authorities on birds believe that all these and other flightless fowl, including penguins, are descended from some very ancient stock that was able to fly. As thousands and millions of years passed, they lost their power of flight, probably because they did not need it. Some kinds, like the kiwi, became smaller. Others, such as the extinct giant moas and elephant birds, grew to a height of ten feet and weighed 1,000 pounds.

What is going to happen to them in the future? No one knows exactly. But the chances are that at some distant time these strange birds, too, will vanish from the earth.

The non-flying kiwis hide during the day and hunt at night.

Australia, which is many times larger than any other island in the South Pacific region, is especially noted for its peculiar beasts. Most of the land is rather flat and often desert-like. Near the east coast, however, there is a long range of mountains with enormous stretches of rich grass land sloping up to them. The northern part is tropical and the rest is subtropical.

One of Australia's most appealing little mammals is the koala, a natural-born teddy bear. It is a gentle, woolly, slow-moving creature with big fringed ears and no tail that you can see. Its long-clawed feet are almost like hands. This fits the koala perfectly for climbing around in the lofty trees where he spends most of his time. The general color of the koala's fur is an odd

The mother's back is the real home of the baby koala.

sort of gray. This is lighter around the cheeks and on the under sides of the ears and throat.

A female usually has only one baby every two years. As soon as the little fellow is born, he enters his mother's fur-lined stomach pouch, which is much like that of a kangaroo. But he does not live there nearly so long as a young kangaroo. Perhaps this is because there are fewer natural enemies in the tree-tops where the koala stays than on the ground where the kangaroo must stay.

Just the same, a koala youngster takes no chances of getting into trouble. When he finally leaves his mother's pouch, she places him on her back. There he instinctively clings tightly to her thick fur. After a while he tries a little cautious creeping. As the weeks pass, he becomes confident enough to climb down her sides and back again. But her back remains his real home until he is fully able to take care of himself.

So far as we know, koalas eat only the leaves and young twigs of eucalyptus trees. Sometimes these trees are 150 feet tall or more. Yet a koala often climbs to their tops for a meal.

A strange thing happens when the time comes for a young koala to change from his mother's milk to a plain eucalyptus diet. Every two or three days, for about a month, her body produces a sort of eucalyptus soup. Apparently this occurs only at a special time in the afternoon. The soup is easily digested and helps the little fellow make the change-over to raw twigs and leaves.

All mammals which, like the koala and kangaroo, carry their young around in pouches are called *marsupials*. The principal one which we have here in the United States is the Virginia opossum. This peculiar cat-size beast has a prehensile, ratlike tail. It is common in the eastern half of the country from the Canadian border to Florida and the Gulf of Mexico.

Scientists think that marsupials originated in the

All About Strange Beasts of the Present

Northern Hemisphere and migrated from there to the equatorial and other southern regions. They may have reached Australia by land during the ancient days when that island was connected with southern Asia and a land bridge joined northeastern Asia with North America.

Australia and the islands near it have more kinds of marsupials than any other part of the world. Some are very small and burrow in the ground like mice and moles. Others are carnivorous and look like big dogs. Certain kinds resemble flying squirrels. And there are many other types. The kangaroo group alone has 129 species and subspecies.

Some of the especially interesting 'roos, as the Australians call kangaroos, are tree-dwellers. These are much smaller than the wallabies and large kangaroos that you often see in our zoos. Also, their hind legs are much shorter and their tails more slender. They can get around all right on the ground, but they spend most of their time high in the trees. Their long, slim tails are not prehensile. Probably the tail's most important job is helping the 'roo keep his balance in shaky places. It is likely that the tail is also used as a sort of rudder when making long leaps from branch to branch. Finally, a tree kangaroo clamps his tail, like a prop, against the bark when climbing the trunk of a big tree.

These surprising tree 'roos live in the mountain rain forests of northeastern Australia. Many of the trees there grow very tall, but the beasts climb to their very tops to feed on fruits or leaves, or to escape from some enemy. They can leap forty feet through the air to a somewhat lower limb. Occasionally they drop almost straight down to a heavy limb thirty feet below them. When chased out of a tree by a man, they dive to the ground, bounce up and leap away at good speed.

This sort of treetop life requires special leg and foot

In Australia certain kinds of kangaroos live in trees.

equipment, of course. So a tree kangaroo's front legs and feet are much larger and stronger, for his size, than those of a land-dwelling species. The feet have strong, sharp claws which can get a first-class grip on branches of all sizes. Also, their soles have rough pads to cushion the jolt when the 'roo lands on a heavy limb or perhaps the ground.

Tree kangaroos are not often seen because they stay well hidden among the leaves of their favorite trees. Some natives of Australia hunt them successfully, though, with the help of a keen-nosed dog. When the dog scents one in a tree, his master climbs up and either scares or drags it to the ground.

The What-Is-It

I think everyone will agree that the duckbilled platypus is the strangest living beast in Australia—or anywhere else. Scientists and other people argued for many years about whether it was related to birds, mammals or reptiles. Modern zoologists, however, have finally decided that it is a sort of link connecting the mammals with mammal-like reptiles that flourished about 180,000,000 years ago during the Triassic Period.

It is easy to understand all this confusion when you

know what the platypus is like. A fully grown male is about two feet long, and a female is a few inches shorter. One-fourth of the length is tail. The beasts are covered with short, velvety, grayish-brown fur. Their small eyes and ears are provided with a sort of furrow that buries them completely when the platypuses are under water. The duckbill part of the name comes from their incredible jaws. These are leathery, pliable, and fitted with roughnesses along the gums which take

The duckbilled platypus is the strangest beast of all.

the place of teeth. The two nostrils are well forward on the upper side of the top jaw. The whole fantastic arrangement strongly resembles a broad duck's beak.

Then there are those astonishing front feet. These are rounded and wider than they are long. Their extra-size webs extend well beyond the tips of the long claws. When a platypus digs its home burrow in the ground, these flappy parts of the webs are folded underneath to get them out of the way. The smaller hind feet are webbed, too, but all the toes are curved sideways. A full-grown male has a hard, dangerously poisonous spur at the base of each hind foot. Both males and females use their bunched hind toes to comb their glossy fur coats!

Platypuses are found in eastern Australia and the nearby island of Tasmania. Their range extends from almost sea level to a height of 6,000 feet in the mountains. They always live close to streams, lakes or water holes. This is because they get all their food under water.

When a platypus decides to get a meal, it submerges and rummages around in the muddy bottom as though it were really a duck. There it finds worms, aquatic insects, crayfish and other tasty bits. Generally it returns to the surface in a minute or so to get a fresh breath and chew whatever delicacies it has caught. Then down it goes again for another minute of puddling.

For a creature that weighs only two to four pounds, the platypus has an amazing appetite. There is one record of a captive female that ate a pound and three-quarters of grubs, earthworms and crayfish in a single night. She was nursing her baby at the time, which probably increased her ordinary hunger.

Platypuses spend much of the time in burrows which they dig with their front feet in the bank above the surface of the water. The nesting tunnel, which is dug entirely by the female, may be anywhere from 15 to 60 or even 100 feet long. She enlarges it at the end to make room for a floor lining of grass, leaves and sometimes twigs.

In this nest she lays one, two or sometimes three whitish, leathery-shelled eggs much like those of regular reptiles. Before doing this she plugs up the tunnel behind her with several earth walls six inches or more thick. This is to shut out enemies and perhaps keep the air in the nest properly damp.

The eggs, warmed by her body as she curls herself

around them, hatch in less than two weeks. A few days later milk starts to ooze out of large pores in her skin. Then the babies begin to suck it from her fur.

Young platypuses cannot open their eyes for about eleven weeks after they are hatched. Altogether, they stay in the nest for nearly seventeen weeks before coming out and entering the water.

Yes, the duckbilled platypus is certainly the strangest strange beast of the present!

6

The Web
of Life

Perhaps you are surprised by the terrific differences between the queer creatures which you have met in these pages. Some of them weigh tons and others only ounces. Their coats may consist of fur, feathers, scales or plain slippery skin. They eat almost anything you can think of except stones. Among them are beauty and ugliness, brightness and stupidity, gentleness and ferocity, speed and unbelievable clumsiness. Their homes range all the way from dark ocean depths to glittering mountaintops.

One important reason for the astonishing differences between these and countless other beasts is that every form of life, anywhere in the world, depends upon other forms of life. A mountain sheep would die without his meals of plant parts. Plants could not exist if there were not billions of helpful microscopic creatures in the soil around their roots. These tiny bacteria, in turn, would perish without the presence of water, air and certain chemical elements. These chemical elements come partly from plant leaves and stems which are returned to the soil after having been eaten by the mountain sheep. It is a sort of circle, or wheel, which never stops turning.

There are untold millions of such "wheels" on the lands and in the waters of the globe. All must continue to turn, for if they stopped the whole plan would begin to fall apart. Each of them is suited to the particular climate in which it operates. And, as you know, there are many, many different climates and environments!

No one knows the full details of this colossal "web of life" which spreads over the earth. Not even our topmost scientists have all the answers to its mysteries. But it is very exciting to peep between its meshes here and there, as you explore the wonders of plant and animal life.

Index

Index

United States, animals of, on land,
9ff., 81, 135
  in water, 25ff.
changes of climate in, 5
desert oddities of, 47-53
fossil remains of walrus in, 55

Vampire bat, 100-02
Vertebrate animals, first, 35

Virginia opossum, 135

Walrus, 55-57
Weasel, 9
Whale, killer, 60
  sperm, 39, 40, 41
Wolf, as enemy of muskox, 61, 62
Wolverine (skunk-bear), 9-11, 12,
15